THE
SELF EMPLOYED
MORTGAGE
GUIDE

GARY DAS

R3THINK PRESS

First published in Great Britain 2017
by Rethink Press (www.rethinkpress.com)

Gary Das professional compliance statement

I have a company called Active Brokers Limited.

The mortgage advice process is unique to the client and their own circumstances, so the information in this book does not constitute advice. It is for information purposes only.

You should always contact a mortgage adviser for personalised advice for your specific circumstances. Please ask for a personalised illustration if you require one.

A fee of up to 2% of the mortgage amount may be payable. The precise amount will depend on your circumstances. A typical example would be £995.00 payable on application and the remainder payable on mortgage offer. We will also be paid commission from the lender.

Active Brokers Limited is authorised and regulated by the Financial Conduct Authority and is entered on the Financial Services Register (http://www.fca.org.uk/register) under reference 488342. The Financial Conduct Authority does not regulate business buy-to-let mortgages, or most commercial mortgages.

Your home may be repossessed if you do not keep up repayments on your mortgage.

You may have to pay an early repayment charge to your existing lender if you re-mortgage.

The following information is correct as at July 2017.

Praise

Gary Das is a well-known, well respected mortgage broker, and this publication could not have been written by a more well-informed individual. Gary and his team have worked with thousands of customers over the years, not only to educate them, but to enable them to apply for loans successfully. This book has a clear, simple formula to help the self-employed achieve a mortgage. I also found in it some great hints and tips on property, business – and life in general! When you need advice, seek assistance from an expert. This book is exactly that.

Mark Wright, Director, Climb Online, winner of *The Apprentice* in 2014

Gary Das is part of Entrepreneur's Network and an expert mortgage broker who helps our members. He has taken all his knowledge and set it out in a simple step-by-step guide to help every self-employed person to prepare their mortgage application and acquire their dream home. The book contains detailed, practical information for every entrepreneur, yet is very readable. If you are planning to buy or refinance a property in the next few years, then this is for you.

James Sinclair, owner of Marsh Farm Animal Adventure Park, founder of Entrepreneurs Network

"This is a 'must have' guide for business owners and the self-employed. Gary Das is approachable and straight talking, with unquestionable customer focus. Gary demystifies the sometimes daunting process with his simple ACTIVE step-by-step approach. Using plain language to assist you, from preparation which could start months if not years in advance, to achieving the goal of moving into your dream home with ease, he provides the simple advice that business owners should know the day-to-day numbers of their business to the summary at the end of the guide which I particularly found useful as an aide memoire."

Nigel Brumpton, Restaurateur, Charnallies, Clacton-on-Sea, property investor and landlord, and independent vehicle lease agent

Contents

Part 4: Identify

Part 5: Victory

Part 6: Entrepreneurial

Introduction

If you want your business to make £1m, you generally need to do some preparation, planning, and goal setting. It's no different when it comes to buying your dream property.

As a self-employed sole trader, business owner or entrepreneur, when you decide the time's right to refinance, buy or move to a new property, all you really want is to do it without any added stress, worry or anxiety. Being the people we are, we take the risk of stepping away from the security of employment and potential employer benefits to go at it alone, taking on the endless pursuit of having more time, more money and less stress to do more of the things we love. There are now over 4.76 million[1] self-employed people in the UK (that's

---

1. http://www.ons.gov.uk/employmentandlabourmarket/peoplein work/employmentandemployeetypes/bulletins/uklabourmarket/sep tember2016

approximately one in seven of the working population). I live in Essex, which has over 100,000 self-employed people.[2] Business owners stimulate the economy, form 99.3% of the UK's private sector,[3] bring jobs, and add security for our employees.

But when it comes to applying for a mortgage to buy your dream home, some banks and mortgage lenders can find the way we earn our income confusing. On the high street, lenders generally average our income over two to three years, whereas – hopefully – our businesses will be growing so considering only the most recent year could increase the amount we are able to borrow. Majority of the high-street lenders choose to only consider salary and dividends, even though we may have retained profit that we've decided to leave in the business to make more money and reduce our personal tax bills.

The list of issues you face when approaching a lender direct could seem endless, so it really pays to work with an adviser who fully understands company accounts, tax years and/or limited companies. After all, who wants to add unnecessary stress to their life?

---

2. https://www.nomisweb.co.uk/reports/lmp/la/1941962833/printable.aspx

3. https://www.gov.uk/government/uploads/system/uploads/attachment_data/file/467443/bpe_2015_statistical_release.pdf

Why you should read this book

I believe every business owner, sole trader or entrepreneur can live their dream life and own their dream property; all it takes is a little bit of planning and preparation.

In 2015, I moved home with my family and learnt some valuable lessons during the process, more of which later. I wrote this book to bring all the knowledge I have into one place, so that you don't suffer the anxiety, stress and worry I did when I was rejected by my existing lender back in June 2015.

Once my family was settled in our dream home in October 2015, I reflected on the problems I had faced, the mistakes I had made and having now had success with 100s of applications and spoken to 1000s of self-employed people and company directors about their mortgage needs, I have pieced it all together to come up with a solution to help you, either buy or refinance / remortgage your dream home.

I have designed this book to fit the majority, not the minority, of people. Each lender has a different set of criteria (more on this later) and the more criteria you can meet, the more lenders will be available to you, as well as the option of a larger mortgage and potentially lower interest rates. The more specialist your requirements, the more limited your options may be.

My ethos is to avoid saying no to clients. If it isn't possible for them to refinance, buy or move straight away, then I like to set a date, create a goal, and put a strategy in place to help them achieve that goal. My clients tell me this is what sets me and my team apart from high-street lenders. We really want to say, 'Yes, go for it now!'

If you read this book and find that the information in it does not apply to your circumstances, you should speak to an adviser.

A big problem

A big problem I have with self-employed people is that often they do not know the day-to-day numbers of their business, so this book breaks down the figures you will need to be able to supply to mortgage lenders.

I also find that many self-employed people wait until they have their accounts in hand or hit their year-end targets before starting to think about a mortgage and the dream home or investment property they want! This is not the best method, because it gets in the way of preparation. To buy or live a certain lifestyle takes planning and goal setting 12–24 months in advance.

As a business owner, you will need to consider setting business targets based on:

- the mortgage repayments and your future cost of living
- the deposit and fees to buy, move or invest
- the personal income and business profits needed
- the company expenses and taxes you have to pay
- the sales/turnover you have to achieve to cover all of the above

Once you know these numbers, you can set annual, quarterly, monthly, or even weekly or daily targets to achieve the funds you need.

Success lies in the preparation

If you're like me, all you really want is a secure home for your family – a home full of love, security and contentment that will allow you to focus on your business and enjoy your life. A mortgage is the vehicle most of us have to use to get that home. Whether you're a first-time buyer, or buying your £1m+ home, this book can help you. I've provided some information on finding the right property and on what to do when you own one, so that you can continue your property journey in an entrepreneurial way.

In this book, I'll guide you step by step through what I did, what I should have done, and what I have learnt from helping hundreds of sole traders, company directors and property investors achieve more than £50m in lending to buy their properties since I niched my company in January 2016. I'll tell you my story as I go along, so you know what you'll need when the time comes to either refinance, buy or move house. My goal is to give you straightforward instructions for buying your dream home and improving your chances of achieving the best possible mortgage. By following my ACTIVE framework, all self-employed individuals, business owners and entrepreneurs can experience the same success I did.

The key lies in ample preparation, beginning well before you wish to buy, because a lot of the problems I see revolve around money (more on this later) and the proof of adequate income. I love helping business owners, sole traders and entrepreneurs to achieve their dream lifestyle and property by reverse-engineering the numbers.

If you put the steps in this book into action 12 to 24 months in advance of when you want to buy, your journey could be much less stressful.

Note: If you're a first time buyer, make sure you follow *every* step. Skip a step and you could find yourself in trouble. How your income is presented to a bank or lender could affect how much you can borrow in the future --we'll talk about this in more detail later. (If, on the other hand, you're just moving house or looking for a better mortgage deal, you could skip some of the sections, such as those on interest rates or identifying the right type of property for you.)

A bit about me

I'm both a very family-oriented man and a proud business owner. I'm also a fitness fanatic, because fitness and business share many qualities: dedication, consistency, and passion, to name a few. Nothing brings me greater pleasure than having a great work/life balance. My family, friends and business mean the world to me; everything I do is to give my family the best life possible.

As I was growing up, my father was a huge inspiration and mentor to me (he still is today). He's been running his own businesses for a little over thirty years now and he is probably the biggest factor in me going it alone too. Within twelve months of starting Active Brokers, I met my wife and best friend Ayesha. Almost nine years on, and after six years of marriage, we have two gorgeous girls, with a third little one on the way in 2018.

My primary goal is to provide them with a dream life and to make them proud. With their support, I work extremely hard to give them financial security and the best possible future –without spoiling them, of course.

I started my career at Woolwich Building Society, which was where I passed my Certificate in Mortgage Advice and Practice (CeMAP) exams. I've been qualified to provide mortgage advice since 2002.

I had various roles over the next four years, and in November 2006 I left the security of an employed role to became a sole trader, trading under the name 'Active Mortgage Consultants', which was authorised by a large umbrella-type company, which in turn was authorised and regulated by the then Financial Services Authority.

In March 2008, I set up Active Brokers Limited, and in October 2008 I was granted direct authorisation by the Financial Conduct Authority (FCA) to have more control over my business future. This was a triumph for me, because although I love numbers, a spreadsheet and being analytical, when I left junior school at thirteen (my school was weird) I had a maths age of about nine. It was by far my weakest subject, and throughout my last three years of school and GCSEs I had extra maths lessons every week – something of an irony, as I'm now referred to as the number one mortgage expert for self-employed people!

My own mortgage struggles

Chelmsford in Essex had seen significant increases in property values and when Ayesha and I decided it was a good time to move house in June 2015, I approached my existing lender – only to be surprised at the outcome.

They would only lend us half of what we wanted for our 'forever' home. With Ayesha being a sole trader, they'd only assess our personal income, that is, my salary and dividends as a limited company director along with Ayesha's net profit as a sole trader (more on this later). I got so frustrated because Active Brokers had had a great profit that year and they wouldn't take that into consideration.

In the end, I gave up with them. To be honest, I felt a bit sorry for their mortgage adviser – I gave him such a hard time! But it wasn't his fault; he was an employee, so he had no understanding of how the self-employed operate, and was simply working to the lender's criteria.

I knew there was another way, so I began contacting every lender in the UK to find one that would allow us to buy our dream home. It was a long and arduous process, because 95% of lenders use the same criteria (namely salary and dividends) as the one who had turned us down. I found a handful of lenders who were prepared to consider my net profit along with my salary. I then needed to consider not only the interest rate, but which would be the most cost effective. So after considering the affordability, criteria and terms, I found a winning lender – and they said 'yes'!

I was able to move my family to our dream home in October 2015 – a very happy and proud moment! Having lived here for almost two years, I can say it really is perfect and provides everything we need while our girls go through school. Having achieved my dream home allows me to focus on helping every one of the 4.76 million self-employed people in the UK to achieve theirs.

> **NOTE:** if you're a business owner, i.e. a limited company director with more than 15–20% of the shares in the company, the majority of lenders classify you as self-employed.

The A C T I V E framework

I'd been in business for nine years when I decided to move house in 2015. The decision turned out to be the best move I've ever made, because having spent seven of those years focused on insurance after the credit crunch, it brought me back to my passion of helping people to buy property and changing their lives. I love solving problems, and I found my niche in self-employed mortgages. Through developing this work I gained a wealth of knowledge that can make your life and the process of buying or moving to a new house as simple and easy as possible.

Let me introduce you to the ACTIVE frame work. It's my own personal method for all self-employed individuals, business owners and entrepreneurs to follow to improve the chances of achieving the same mortgage success as I did. So what does 'ACTIVE' stand for? Let me show you...

A ffordability

Preparing your accounts and income figures is the first and most important step along, with working out your budget to make sure your mortgage is affordable both now and in the future.

Criteria

Every lender assesses income differently, but the goal is the same: to make sure it's sustainable for the long term. I lay out the information you need to be sure your income is ready to present. This may link back to setting business and income targets for your business.

Terms

There are many different products on the market, so understanding the options and choosing the right one are very important. Getting your initial acceptance from the lender and knowing what documents you'll need will allow you to make a detailed application.

Identify

Hunting for the right property can be tricky, and I've learnt some valuable lessons to help you find the right one for you, with regards to type and location, and show you how to make money from it.

Victory

Once you have submitted an application, the main goal is to obtain your full and final acceptance – the mortgage offer. I talk you through the next steps of exchange and completion, and advise on how to speed up the solicitor part of the process.

Entrepreneurial

You can make a lot of money from property, so I share some key actions you can take to do this, and to improve your property for future benefit.

The ACTIVE framework brings clarity to the confusion to help your mortgage application to victory, and offers some valuable lessons on how to begin being entrepreneurial with your property once you've bought it.

Why do I care?

I love to help, solve problems and make other people's lives easier and better. I love business, and working with self-employed people to 'beat' the lenders is my goal.

For quite a few of my clients, as for me, it is not the lender who is the problem, it is their different sets of criteria and applying to the wrong lender for your circumstances that causes difficulties. Fortunately for you, I'm highly competitive, so every mortgage application is a chance to win – and you *can* win if you start to prepare and think ahead.

I've faced the same problems you may face on your mortgage journey and I've tried to put all the answers you need in this guide to help you get the property of your dreams, so it can become a reality. I want you to have the same feeling I did when my mortgage application was finally accepted; nothing brings me greater pleasure than helping people succeed. This has nothing to do with the mortgage itself; it is all about family, safety, security, changing lives and achieving dreams.

PART 1

Affordability

My Story
STARTING OUT

In 2006, I bought my first property, as single lad, about one month after I went self-employed. For some, it wouldn't be considered the brightest move, but I knew I could make it work and I wanted to be completely in charge of my own destiny.

I bought a flat right before the credit crunch struck, while I was still employed as a mortgage adviser – at the same time that Northern Rock was offering 100% mortgages, that is, mortgages with no deposit. Having bought the flat at the peak of the property prices, I spent a fair bit of time in negative equity, meaning that the flat was worth way less than the outstanding mortgage.

In 2008, I met Ayesha. We got married in 2011 and planned to have children almost straight after. We knew straight away we wanted to move from a flat into a house. We agreed that we'd buy a house we'd live in for five years and then reassess our lives.

At that time, Ayesha was employed and she'd managed to save a deposit, as she'd lived at home. We decided to work out how much we could borrow; at that time it involved using income multiples, which I'll touch on later. We considered the monthly cost along with the prospected costs for our future child and set about finding the lowest interest rate and getting an agreement in principle. It was much simpler to get a mortgage at that time, as we used my salary and dividend from my business, along with an employed income.

By 2014, we had two daughters and the subject of schools cropped up – we hadn't considered schools when we bought together in 2011. By this time Chelmsford house prices had really recovered and things were on the up, so I suggested moving, but we knew once our first daughter started school we'd stick within a certain area, to avoid her having to change schools.

When we looked at the value of our property, we were shocked by how much it had shot up. I'd put the mortgage on the shortest term possible – the shorter the mortgage term, the less interest you pay and we were sitting on a nice amount of equity.

We looked at houses and had an idea in our minds of what we wanted. We considered areas where we could see ourselves for the next ten to fifteen years while our girls went through their school years. It made sense financially, too: my business had made a great profit that year so every box was ticked.

As I knew the amount of equity I had, I sat down to work out the deposit we could afford, bearing in mind all the costs of moving, including:

- solicitor's fees
- stamp duty
- valuations and surveys
- paying off our debts to put us in the best financial position
- removal costs

The mortgage goalposts had moved since we had bought our first place. The industry had tightened up. The income multiples I had used during my career had been removed and replaced with new affordability checks, which means lenders have a responsibility to check your overall income and expenditure to see how much you can borrow.

Chapter 1
PREPARING YOURSELF

After deciding you want to buy a house, move to a new one, the next logical step is to figure out what mortgage you can afford – but don't just assume you're going to get a mortgage.

The number of people I've spoken to who've agreed a sale on their current property and/or placed an offer on a new property before even considering whether they can get a mortgage is shocking. They're going ahead with buying a house with no guarantee that a lender will even give them the money they need. The first step should always be to work out how much you can afford, then working out how much you can borrow.

The thing about affordability is that there's no 'one size fits all'. Five different lenders can offer five different mortgage amounts using the exact same income figures, as they all have their own interpretation of affordability. Affordability is based on your total income and expenditure. This includes regular outgoings, such as food and utilities, debts, travel, cost of dependents and your projected mortgage payments.

The good news is that you can get a rough idea yourself with a bit of homework. Going through your personal circumstances will help you to prepare yourself and get an understanding of what you can borrow.

In the next section, I'm going to teach how to review your own affordability and what you need to consider so you can assess your own mortgage ahead of time and set yourself up for success. When you pass the affordability checks, you're taking a significant step towards getting your mortgage.

Understanding affordability can also help you to get your dream home rather than just any old home, because knowing what lenders are looking for will help you to increase your borrowing power.

Calculating how much you can borrow

As a self-employed person, your income could come from a number of different sources. Mortgage lenders want to make sure your income is sustainable and will continue for the term of the mortgage. They will also go through your bank statements to check your income and expenditure as part of the application process – more on this later.

The basics

First, let's go over some of the basics that affect how lenders see your affordability. To calculate your affordability, take your total monthly income (after tax) and subtract your monthly outgoings (everything you pay out for bills, gyms, loans, credit card, entertainment, etc.). The amount remaining is your disposable income, that is, the amount you can spend. Your monthly mortgage and necessary insurance premiums must fit within this figure.

Affordability example

£6,000 monthly net income – £4,000 outgoings = £2,000 disposable income, so the maximum mortgage repayment and insurance premiums must be less than £2,000, but you should add some sort of buffer for contingencies, so call it £1,600–1,800.

The other term sometimes used for your monthly repayment is your mortgage budget.

This calculation is the most important part of your mortgage application. If you don't have any disposable income, you won't be able to afford a mortgage.

When looking at your affordability the key is to assess on your current *and* future costs. Work through how your expenditure looks now and then do exactly the same for the future.

Note: when looking at future expenditure or considering moving, make sure you remove your current mortgage or rent costs, otherwise your figures will not be accurate.

First-time buyer's tip

I know from my own properties that the cost of owning a flat compared with that of owning a four-bedroom house are very different, not least because expenses like council tax and home insurance are relative to the property and the postcode. One thing you can do is to ask friends and family for some idea of what they are paying.

To download your own budget planner visit: www.activebrokers.co.uk/book

Deposit

The other necessity for buying a house is having money available for a deposit.

Long gone are the days when you could get a 100% mortgage, that is, putting down no deposit and having the entire mortgage to repay.

Note: The information above is correct at the time of writing this book, but things may change, so it is always best to seek advice from an adviser.

As at July 2017, there's one lender in the UK that will offer you a mortgage with no deposit. However, your family or friends will need to have the funds to provide 10% of the property's purchase price, to be placed into a savings account with the lender. Your family get their money back with interest providing you keep up with your repayments for the first three years. Speak to an adviser about your personal circumstances to find out if this is relevant to you.

In any other circumstances, you will need a 5% deposit as a minimum and some lenders will want to see proof of it being available at the point of application, so bear this in mind when you are doing your preparation.

The first step towards acceptance for a mortgage is an agreement in principle (which I will touch on later). The mortgage lender will complete a credit check and may request that you increase your deposit. This is what happened to Ayesha and me when we bought our first house together: we applied with a 5% deposit, and the lender came back and requested a 10% deposit before they would lend to us. Lenders have their own criteria, but a general rule of thumb is that the more deposit you have the greater chance you have of being accepted – or at least, that is my personal impression.

If you can save a 10%+ deposit, you will have a greater choice of mortgage lenders.

It's worth noting that a larger deposit also improves the interest rate. You'll generally see interest rates decrease with deposits of 15%, 20%, 25% and 35%. However, don't let this hold you up when it comes to buying a property. If you have a deposit saved, seek advice about your personal circumstances.

First-time buyer's tip

Property value £500,000, 10% deposit = £50,000

There are several other fees you need to pay when you apply for a mortgage, so you have to budget for these alongside your deposit. Lenders will want to see in your application that you have the money available for these extras.

Most lenders will not let you fund your deposit through personal loans or credit cards, but there is at present one lender who will allow this, providing it fits with their affordability calculation. Remember, it is the lender's overall responsibility to assess income and expenditure, so make sure your application is consistent with the affordability you calculated in the previous section. Seek advice from an adviser about your personal circumstances if this is something you want to do.

Gifted deposits

A deposit can be gifted to you for the purpose of buying a home but with one massive caveat: majority of lenders will not allow the deposit be gifted by someone who is going to live with you and not be party to the mortgage (unless it is your partner). I haven't yet found a lender who will accept that.

Generally, most lenders accept a gifted deposit from someone who is related to you by:

- blood
- marriage

- common-law partnership, or
- civil partnership

There is a small number of lenders who will accept a deposit from anyone, so it is best to seek advice from an adviser if this is you and approaching one of these lenders will help.

A wife was applying for the mortgage in her own name; her husband wasn't going on the mortgage. The deposit was being gifted by his parents, but as the couple were married that was acceptable.

I had another client who was buying his parent' house with his wife, and the parents were gifting the deposit. The house was worth £350,000 and the parents were gifting £35,000, so they applied for a mortgage of £315,000. This is called a concessionary purchase as no money physically changes hands.

I must stress that the family member can't hold any interest in the property following completion of the mortgage – the gift would not be acceptable if they were going to live in the property.

Your adviser should provide you with the relevant lender's gifted deposit template letter. The purpose of this letter is to confirm that the money being gifted is indeed a non-repayable gift, and that the donors will not be party to the mortgage – that is, that the money in question is not a loan.

Government house purchase schemes

Government house purchase schemes were available at the time of writing the book, but check with your adviser about whether they are still available and about your circumstances. (There are other schemes I have not covered, but I have chosen the most common and those I have most experience with.)

Help to Buy ISA

If you're saving to buy your first home, you could save money into a Help to Buy ISA (individual savings account). The Government will boost your savings by 25%, so for every £200 you save, you'll receive a government bonus of £50. The maximum government bonus you can receive is £3,000. The Help to Buy ISA is available from a range of banks, building societies and credit unions.

The accounts are available to every first-time buyer, and are not limited to one per household. This means if you're planning to buy with your partner, you could receive a government bonus of up to £6,000 towards your first home. If more than two of you are applying, it is best to speak to an adviser or the Help to Buy agent to confirm the situation at that time.

You can save up to £200 a month in your Help to Buy ISA. To kick-start your account, you can deposit a lump sum of up to £1,200 in the first month.

The minimum government bonus is £400, which means you need to have saved at least £1,600 before you can claim your bonus. The maximum government bonus available is £3,000 so you will need to have saved £12,000 to receive it.

When you're close to buying your first home, you'll need to instruct your solicitor or conveyancer to apply for your government bonus. Once they receive the government bonus, it will be added to the money you're putting towards your first home.

The bonus must be included with the funds consolidated at the completion of the property transaction and can't be used for the deposit due at the exchange of contracts, to pay for solicitor's, estate agent's fees, or any other indirect costs associated with buying a house.

See more details here: https://www.helptobuy.gov.uk/help-to-buy-isa/how-does-it-work

Equity loan

The government lends you up to 20% of the cost of a newly built home. It means you'll only need a 5% cash deposit and a 75% mortgage to make up the rest. You won't be charged fees on the 20% loan for the first five years of owning your home.

If you want to own a newly built home in London, you could borrow up to 40% of the purchase price from the Government with the London Help to Buy scheme. You would only need a 5% deposit and your mortgage would make up the rest.

This offer is only available on properties up to £600,000, and you cannot own an existing property. This means that if you are moving, you will have to sell your existing property first.

You will also have cheaper monthly mortgage payments, because they will be based on 75% of the purchase price rather than 95% i.e. the government after gifting you 20%.

Speak to an adviser about whether this is the right option for you. For more information visit: https://www.helptobuy.gov.uk/ and https://www.helptobuylondon.co.uk/

Shared ownership

Shared ownership means that you don't buy complete ownership of the property. You buy a share, that is, 60% of the property, and you rent the remaining 40%. This can make larger properties more affordable, and most shared ownership schemes offer you the chance to buy additional shares in future years.

If you are considering shared ownership, you do need to know the rent being charged for the share, along with the total of any property maintenance costs, so you can factor these into your affordability calculations.

Example

- Mortgage payment: £500 per month
- Rent payable for shared ownership: £250 per month
- Ground rent and/or service charges: £80 per month

For more information visit: https://www.helptobuy.gov.uk/shared-ownership

Seek advice from an adviser about your personal circumstances and affordability if this is something you want to pursue.

Cost of buying and moving

In addition to raising a deposit, you'll need to be able to cover the costs of buying and moving into your new home.

The main things to consider are:

- Solicitors: the costs of using solicitors depends on the value of the house. On average, the fee for buying a house is somewhere between £1,300– £1,500. If you're buying a house and selling your current property, you can usually expect to double this cost.[1]
- Stamp duty: This is a tax based on the price of the house. As you can see in the table below, it is applied through a tiered structure. For example, if your property was worth £500,000 you'd pay no tax on the first £125,000, you'd pay 2% on the next £125,000, and 5% on the remaining amount. As it goes through the tiers, you add on the tax.

---

1. https://www.moneyadviceservice.org.uk/en/articles/estimate-your-overall-buying-and-moving-costs

Property value	Stamp duty land tax (SDLT)[2]
Up to £125,000	Zero
From £125,001 to £250,000 (the next £125,000)	2%
From £250,001 to £925,000 (the next £675,000)	5%
From £925,001 to £1.5m (the next £575,000)	10%
Above £1.5m	12%

- Valuation, homebuyer's or full structural survey (valuations available for the property you wish to buy): You'll need to budget for up to £1,000, as it's dependent on the value of the property. I'll expand on these later.
- Miscellaneous: there could be a few other fees like telegraphic transfer fees, adviser fees, application fee, and booking fees, all of which we will come to later. You need to allow up to £2, 000 or so for these.

Unfortunately, there's no way to get round these fees and some of them can't be added to the mortgage.

I know you are probably itching to know how much you can borrow; that is coming up in the 'criteria' section, but there is still some important information to cover first.

---

2. As at tax year 2017/2018

Fact-finding process

I'm going to show you what to be aware of and how lenders view your circumstances when deciding how much you can borrow.

Mortgages are an advice-based product, which means that under the regulatory guidelines of the Financial Conduct Authority (FCA) any adviser or lender has to 'know their client'. This is done by completing a 'fact find'. The information gathered during this exercise is used to provide bespoke advice and a personalised recommendation for the right lender, product and interest rate.

An initial consultation with a mortgage adviser will involve a fact-finding strategy session, where your adviser will discuss your:

- personal information and circumstances
- outstanding debts (if any)
- monthly income and outgoings
- aspirations
- attitude to risk

Although this process sounds boring, it is essential, and that's why every financial service organisation in the UK will put you through it. My job is to fly through it as quickly as possible, capturing all the key information about you and your business, because this is the information that is going to be presented to a lender as part of your mortgage application.

The process can take anywhere from thirty minutes to an hour, depending on your circumstances. It can be done face-to-face or over the phone. If you're looking to make rapid progress, a phone call is usually your best option. This is the first step to starting your application and moving you closer to your mortgage offer.

The more detailed and honest you are, the better the advice your adviser can provide, and the greater your chances of mortgage success. Remember, if they're basing their advice on incorrect or missing information, or presenting this to a mortgage lender, it could harm your application.

After the fact-finding is complete, an adviser will draw up a plan that is tailored to your circumstances. My team include recommendations on the most suitable:

- lender
- mortgage type
- interest rate
- the protection you'll need – life insurance, critical illness and income protection and home insurance

The adviser will want to get a realistic picture of the monthly expenditure you are committed to, now and in the future, so let's look at what they'll take into account.

Dependants

According to a recent survey by Liverpool Victoria, it costs £231,843 to bring up a child until their twenty-first birthday.[3] Although no lender actually confirms how dependents affect

---

3. https://www.lv.com/life-insurance/cost-of-a-child The 'cost of a child' calculations', from birth to 21 years, were compiled by the Centre of Economic and Business Research (CEBR) for LV= in December 2015 and are based on the cost for the 21-year period to December 2015.

your affordability, what we have seen with most lenders is that the more children you have, the more it affects the amount you can borrow.

As well as the number of children, the majority of lenders usually factor into your affordability:

- childcare costs
- school and nursery fees
- regular clubs/membership costs i.e. after-school clubs, gymnastic, dance etc.
- maintenance payments

I have never paid a day's childcare, as we are lucky to have grandparents available, and a strong network of family and friends who can help out. If you both work full time and don't declare childcare as an expense, some lenders will want an explanation as to who is looking after your children.

Another type of dependent is anyone who lives with you but isn't on the mortgage application, such as an elderly relative. For some lenders this could reduce your affordability, as they might assume that your relative entails extra costs for your household, for example, increased electricity bills and higher food costs. Even if your relative has an income, if they are not party to the mortgage, this income will not be taken into account. In these situations I would seek advice from an adviser.

Maintenance

If you have children from a previous relationship and are paying maintenance for them, this will also be factored into your affordability. Maintenance payments can also be factored into affordability as a source of income, so whether you pay or receive maintenance could increase or lower your affordability: seek advice.

Debts

In the 'good old days' before the 2008 credit crunch, it was really easy to factor debts into your monthly expenditure and calculate how much you could borrow. Now each lender's affordability calculator does this for me. Your job is to be honest about everything, as it will show up at credit score stage anyway.

It really helps if you have your credit report, because it outlines exactly the information an adviser needs to be able to factor in your debts. If you have any of the following, it will need to be declared as part of your agreement in principle, more on this later:

- loans
- credit cards
- hire purchase or personal contract purchase overdrafts
- family debts

The considerations for lenders include:

- Will the debt/s be present after the completion of the new mortgage and you're living in your home?
- If you're selling a property and repaying debts from

the equity, will there be a sufficient amount left for a deposit afterwards?

- If you're clearing debts from savings, do you have enough to cover them along with the deposit, stamp duty, and other mortgage related fees?

To answers these questions, lenders may request to see proof of adequate funds. If, for example, you're moving house and clearing your debts from the equity in your home, most lenders won't include your current monthly repayments in their affordability checks and therefore you could borrow more. If you are able to settle your debts before applying for a mortgage, this could also help you a great deal.

Once your debts are clear, it can take a few weeks for your credit report to update.

Factoring in remaining debts: If, on the other hand, you have a debt you want to keep after your new mortgage has completed, there is a quick way to factor it into how much you can borrow.

The following are only examples for you to use as 'homework', and it is best to speak to an adviser to get an accurate mortgage amount specific to your circumstances. Remember, lenders have a responsibility to assess income and expenditure. (These examples will make more sense in the next section, when you work out how much you can borrow.)

Credit cards/overdrafts: Take the balance of your credit card or overdraft and multiply it by 3% to obtain the minimum monthly repayment. If the balance on your credit card is £1,000, 3% of it is £30 per month.

Loans, HP, PCP (anything with an agreement monthly payment): Imagine you also have a loan at £300 per month. Take the annual total and subtract it from your annual income, as shown below.

Example

Credit card: £30 per month × 12 = £360 per annum.
Loan: £300 per month × 12 = £3600 per annum.
Income: £30,000 − (£360 + £3600) = £26,040

With my quick calculation, it is the remaining income after the deduction of your monthly debt repayments that we will use for the basis of how much you can borrow.

Debts on behalf of your business: If you've taken out a loan or credit card personally, but are using it for business, some lenders may still include it within your affordability. This could reduce the amount you can borrow. If this is the case, you should get a letter from your company accountant to confirm that it's for the business only and that the cost is factored into your company accounts. If you're doing this please seek advice from an adviser.)

Note: If you're clearing personal debt from your business bank account, it can help to get a letter from your accountant to confirm that the business can afford to have the amount in question withdrawn from it and that this isn't going to have a detrimental effect on your business's financial position. Some lenders may also require a business bank statement to show the business has adequate money in the account.

Occupational deductions: The only occupational deductions that are really applicable to self-employed people are student loans. These are factored into affordability and reduce the amount you can borrow.

Employed: any items listed on your pay slip could, as far as most lenders are concerned, have a negative effect on the amount you can borrow. This includes things like:

- student loans
- travel costs
- pension contributions
- health care/insurance
- share schemes (although these may provide income later they are a cost now)

Some lenders will take the view that these are optional and therefore can be excluded from the affordability, which could increase the amount you can borrow.

This is something your mortgage adviser will usually consider when providing you with advice based on your circumstances and the amount you need to borrow.

Overdraft

I am surprised by the number of self-employed people and business owners using their overdrafts for day-to-day expenses. I feel this is a problem for mortgage lenders because, from their perspective, this is 'living beyond your means'.

IMPORTANT TIPS: Do not go over your overdraft limit as this will significantly reduce your chances of success. If you not have an overdraft and go into a negative balance, you are also significantly reducing your chances. When you apply to a lender, they will review a full three months' bank statements, and in some instances six months', so avoiding overdraft usage for three to six months leading up to your mortgage application could increase your chances.

You could still be accepted for a mortgage even if you have an overdraft, so speak to an adviser about your circumstances.

Mortgage terms and retirement

The term of your mortgage, i.e. the number of years it will run for, has a big impact on the amount you can borrow, as will your age.

The formula goes like this:

1. the longer the mortgage term...
2. ...the lower the mortgage payment...
3. ...the more you could afford monthly
4. = the more you could borrow

Ideally, you want to repay the mortgage before you reach retirement age, which for most people in the UK is currently sixty-eight. (For us self-employed entrepreneurial folk, going on till seventy is viable and usually realistic.)

Right now, it could be possible to run a mortgage up to

the age of eighty-five. However, this can be difficult, because, once you are over the age of seventy, lenders usually want to see proof of income that's enough to afford the mortgage payments. Going past seventy, therefore, has a knock-on effect to the amount you could borrow, so if this is something you are thinking about seek advice.

One of the main reasons for keeping your mortgage on the shortest term possible is that it can drastically reduce the amount of overall interest you pay on your mortgage.

Your goals

Generally lenders are interested in a self-employed person's income over the previous one to three years. However, depending on how far the business is into the current tax year, the lender may ask for forecast end-of-year accounts for the current financial year or even the future financial year, to make sure the business is stable and your income sustainable.

I would hope you have short and long term goals as a business owner. These could affect the advice provided by an adviser and the terms available to you. Some key questions to consider are:

- Do you plan to expand the business?
- Might your income change in the foreseeable future? (three to seven years)
- Might your expenditure change in the foreseeable future? (three to seven years)

- Would you like to make extra mortgage payments or reduce your mortgage with a lump sum payment?
- Are you likely to pay off some or all of the mortgage in the foreseeable future (three to seven years)?
- Are you likely to move in the foreseeable future (three to seven years)?

If you've been turned down . . .

. . . there will be a reason why. However, there may be some options for putting it right. Firstly, an adviser needs to know the lender you applied to and what happened. Was it your credit score, affordability, or something missing from your accounts?

If there was a simple mistake in the way your information was presented, you may have a greater chance of success the second time round with a different lender. Of course, there's no guarantee that every situation in which a client is declined can be resolved.

Some common concerns for clients I have spoken to are:

- I'm newly self-employed
- I'm starting a new limited company after being self-employed sole trader for many years
- I had a loss in my previous tax year
- I don't want to withdraw all my profits just to get a mortgage and pay higher rate tax
- I've had previous self-certified mortgages
- high-street banks have turned me down
- high-street banks won't lend me anywhere near enough

- I'm a contractor (whether a sole operator or via an umbrella organisation)
- I've multiple sources of income
- I want to let my existing home and move into a new one
- I want to buy more property but my portfolio is now my only source of income
- I own a plot of land and want to develop it
- I want to buy commercial premises

If you want to increase your chances of success, preparation is vital, the sooner the better.

Self-employment

Being self-employed can get you the same mortgage as everyone else. You just have to jump through more hoops to get it.

An employed person generally has to show three months' pay slips and bank statements, along with proof of deposit, and boom – they're well on the way. For self-employed folk and business owners, it's not that easy. There are many variables; no two businesses are the same.

Some questions to ask yourself about your self-employed status are:

- How long have you been trading? (it would need to be minimum of one year, ideally two and personally I prefer 3)
- Are you a sole trader or a limited company?
- If you're the director of a limited company, the majority of lenders will classify you as self-employed provided you own more than 20% of the company of which

you are a director; if it's less, you're considered to be employed. (This does, however, range from 15–33% ownership across the whole of the market.)

- Are you showing a healthy (and consistent) net profit?
- Do your liabilities outweigh your assets?
- Do you pay yourself with a director's loan?
- Is your income sustainable in the long term?
- Do you have experience in the trade?
- Are you managing your business and personal banking separately?
- Do you have personal loans that are paid for by the business?
- Do you have an accountant (with the right qualifications), rather than a booker keeper?

These are just a few of the considerations I go through with a self-employed person when assessing if now is the right time for them to proceed with a mortgage, and which lender is the most suitable.

There are as many different scenarios as there are business owners. Out of the hundreds of applications the team and I have made for self-employed people since January 2016, each one has taught us something new.

The frustrating thing, which I have experienced first-hand, is that most mortgage lenders will average your income over two years, but I know from experience that there are a couple of lenders who will consider using the latest year only, which if you have increasing profits could increase the amount you can borrow, but I will touch on this a little later in the book.

Case study: overcoming the lender's concerns

The following scenario concerns a recent client who had been turned down three times. This is my presentation to the lender who subsequently made a mortgage offer.

XYZ Ltd started trading in 2014. The company accounts for the first year of trading, ending in 31/01/2015, showed an income for the director of £800 per week, as a consultancy fee paid by his previous owner, ABC Ltd, of which my client was sole shareholder but not a director, is now in liquidation,

It was placed into liquidation by a professional company, as it was poorly directed; and this resulted in my client taking back control of ABC Ltd as a 100% shareholder.

ABC Ltd had a turnover of £900,000 in its last year. My client was advised by the liquidator to liquidate it and merge his business into XYZ Ltd.

XYZ Ltd took over all the trade of ABC Ltd in 2015, which explains why the figures and trade are so different for 2016. The 2016 turnover for XYZ Ltd was projected at £1.5 m.

Hopefully now you can now see what strikes terror into lenders: liquidation.

It's important to present your case correctly to the right lender, with the right explanations.

I'm pleased to say the lender based their assessment on just the most recent year profits and my client now resides in their dream home.

Summary

Work out how much you can afford, taking into account your debts and commitments, i.e. loans, credit cards, hire purchase, etc., itemising your outgoings and regular spend – visit my website for a budget planner.

Ideally you should have a 10% deposit available, though you could get by with a 5% deposit, especially if you are using a government-backed scheme. Remember that gifted deposits ideally need to be from an immediate relative, and non-repayable. If you are considering applying to Help to Buy, or shared ownership or property schemes, speak to the relevant body ideally before approaching an adviser.

Make sure you factor in all the costs of buying or moving;

- solicitors
- stamp duty
- valuation
- lender fees
- broker fees

The fact-finding process with an adviser will take approximately forty-five minutes to one hour. The adviser will need full details of your finances, including

- current balances
- monthly payments
- overdrafts; and
- start and end dates of your financial commitments

Limit your overdraft usage as much as possible as you prepare to apply for a mortgage – ideally get rid of it completely. If you have been declined a mortgage previously, find out the reasons and obtain your credit report to assist your adviser.

Mortgage terms can generally run for 35 years or up to retirement age, whichever is earlier. The shorter the term the more expensive the monthly repayments and the less interest you will pay.

Think about your future, both personally and within your business.

To download the ACTIVE quick reference guide visit: https://activebrokers.co.uk/book/

Chapter 2
INSURANCE

You may be wondering why I'm devoting a whole chapter to what seems like a side issue. The truth is, everybody *needs* insurance but very few people want it.

If you're moving towards making the biggest financial commitment of your personal life, you need to make sure that your family can keep a roof over their heads and that you can still maintain your standard of living if something happens to you. Insurance is really a very important part of the house buying process and the majority of lenders will want the costs of insurance to be factored into your monthly affordability.

If you are the owner of a limited company, there are a few policies that you can pay for through your business. You'll find these at the end of this book, in the section on the entrepreneurial approach to home owning.

Let's take a look at the different kinds of insurance.

Home insurance

Buildings insurance

Protecting your home is extremely important. Legally, you have to insure the building. This is because the mortgage lender owns a large percentage of your house until it's repaid – of course they want to know it's insured. As lenders require you to have this insurance, it's generally included as a condition of a mortgage offer right from the beginning.

If your home is damaged for any one of a variety of reasons, a buildings insurance policy could give a pay-out to cover all the costs. So, when money's tight and disaster strikes – let's say a window gets smashed – you won't have to worry about how you're going to pay for the repairs. Not having buildings insurance could put your home at risk, especially if you can't have damage repaired immediately.

Contents insurance

Contents insurance is easily explained: turn your house upside down and everything that falls out should be covered by contents insurance. The things that don't fall out – the walls, kitchen units, etc. – are already covered by buildings insurance.

While contents insurance is optional, it's certainly wise to have a look at this cover if you want to protect the valuables in your new home. Contents insurance can cover many things, from your new TV to the antique china on your mantelpiece. A pay-out from this policy will cover the cost of repairing or replacing the item if it's damaged or stolen.

Under-insurance

When taking out buildings and contents insurance, you need to make sure you have a realistic evaluation of what is to be covered. If you've got contents insured for £40,000 and you're burgled, when the loss assessor visits after the event and see your contents are actually worth £80,000, you're underinsured by 50%. When the insurance company comes to pay out, the amount they give you is very likely to be only enough to cover 50% of what you need.

Personal insurance

Insuring the people who pay for the house and its contents every month is arguably even more important than home insurance. It's vital to protect your children, and your loved ones, who may inherit the property if the worst should ever happen to you.

None of this insurance is compulsory, but I highly recommend you factor these costs into your monthly budget. The problems that could arise from not being insured by far outweigh the cost of insurance.

Income protection

If you have an accident and you're self-employed, who's going to pay for your mortgage? I know everyone says – and I've said it myself – 'I'm never ill' or 'it won't happen to me'. But sadly it can often happen when you'd least expect it. Every year nearly one million people find themselves unable to work because of a serious illness or injury.[4]

The government will give you less than £300 a month when you're out of work from illness or disability.[5] Would that cover your mortgage? Most probably not. If you're unable to work and therefore can't pay your mortgage, in time you'll lose your house as well as ruin your credit score for any future loans, credit cards, or even mortgages.

This is the least taken-up policy and yet probably the most important. If you had a money machine that sat in your lounge and on the first of every month it spouted out £2,000, wouldn't you insure it against breaking down? I know I would.

So why are you any different? Insure yourself, especially if you're the main earner and have a small number of staff, or if you are the key person in a limited company, meaning that if you didn't make sales or weren't there the business turnover would suffer.

Income protection can pay you a monthly income of up to 55% of your annual salary, after a deferred period, up until your retirement. You either reach the end of the policy or you die…

The key thing is to understand your income. If it's going down, you may be paying too much for your policy: the insurer will only pay out based on what your actual earnings are.

---

4. https://www.moneyadviceservice.org.uk/en/articles/do-you-need-income-protection-insurance
5. https://www.gov.uk/employment-support-allowance/what-youll-get

Critical illness

Critical illness insurance isn't only there to repay the whole mortgage debt; depending on the illness you suffer it can buy you valuable choices.

Everyone knows someone or has at the very least heard of someone who's suffered from cancer. It's estimated that one in two people will suffer from some form of cancer in their lifetime.[6] If there are two of you on your mortgage, I'm sure you can do the maths.

There are currently up to 80 conditions and operations covered by critical illness insurance, depending on which insurer you choose. The main thing is that the 'big four' conditions should be covered: cancer, heart attack, multiple sclerosis and strokes.

Case study: a life-changing accident

From 18-stone bodybuilder to life-changing major back surgery, followed by potentially the rest of his life in a wheelchair (his fight continues) – would you believe that my best friend is now mortgage free?

You could say this is a testament to Ed. He's got a powerful mindset and accepted his situation after his serious fall while on holiday; at no point did he show any negativity. I've seen him flat out in a hospital bed, then slowly extending his leg out of the wheel chair, then returning

---

6. http://www.cancerresearchuk.org/health-professional/cancer-sta tistics#heading-Three

home in December 2015 and starting back at the gym again. Words can't describe how much respect and admiration I've got for his strength of character.

Ed will walk again (although he will say 'might' and won't stop trying) and after such a traumatic event, he doesn't have the worry of paying his monthly mortgage. We made almost forty calls, over four months, to the hospital and to the insurer to make sure he'd receive his payout. And in February 2016, he finally got it.

Ed said this about having insurance which he had a couple of months previously thought about cancelling:

'If I hadn't had life insurance, things would have been very different. I would have had to sell my house, and I would have had to return to work sooner, because money would have been more of a priority than my health and rehabilitation.

'Before my accident I considered cancelling my life insurance policy, because I thought I would never use it – I'm young, what do I need that for?

'Keeping my policy allowed me to keep my house, rehabilitate myself back in to work and a social life in my own time, maintaining my independence. I would recommend life and critical illness insurance to everyone. The price to pay for not having it for you and your family doesn't bear thinking about.'

Children's critical illness

One free benefit offered by insurers is health cover for your child, usually up to the age of eighteen, or until they leave full-time education, depending on the insurer. Children receive almost the same illness cover as adults allowing for variations between insurers. The sum assured is usual 25% of the cover amount or £25,000, whichever is the lower, again depending on the insurer.

This is a great benefit to have, even though I am confident no parent would ever wish to have to draw on it. It offers the assurance that your child would be getting the very best medical care anywhere in the world.

Life insurance

Life insurance is usually the cheapest form of insurance. If one of you died, could the other still afford the mortgage payments on their sole income? Could your family still maintain the lifestyle you want them to have?

I feel life insurance should be compulsory for every home owner with a mortgage in the UK, as there's just too much risk in not having it. If your partner doesn't earn as much as you or is a househusband/wife, then insurance is vitally important.

There are two main options:

- A level term policy that pays out the same amount at any point during the term, i.e. £100,000 would be paid out in Year 1 or Year 20 of a 25-year policy. The advantage is that if your mortgage is £50,000, whenever you claim, you'll have £50,000 to do with as you please.

- A decreasing term policy, which entails cheaper monthly contributions, means the £100,000 reduces over the course of the 25-year mortgage, only leaving enough to repay the mortgage at any given time.

If you're purchasing life insurance as a sole individual and have no dependents, your home will become part of your estate on your death and be left to your next of kin, i.e. your parents. They'd be expected to pay the mortgage until the house is sold.

Family income benefit policy

Before we go any further, I want you to take a step back and consider your budget planner. Look at the future monthly outgoings and subtract the mortgage payment and ask yourself whether your spouse or children could pay this amount every month, remain in the house, and maintain their current standard of living.

One option you've got is to ensure that monthly amount with a family income benefit policy that would pay £x monthly, so they or you could pay the bills.

Monthly outgoings needing to be covered:
Mortgage   £1,000, repaid by life insurance
Living expenses   £750, repaid by family income insurance

You don't necessarily have to insure the whole amount: if two of you are paying the mortgage and bills and your incomes are similar, it might be worth insuring half the monthly expenditure, as your partner's income could cover the other half.

Summary

Please don't have the attitude that 'it won't happen to me'. You have to consider the 'what ifs' and how your family would survive and maintain their standard of living without an income. These are the main forms of insurance available:

- buildings insurance is compulsory and needs to be in place when you exchange contracts
- contents insurance covers everything that would fall out of your house if you turned it upside down
- income protection could provide you with an income in the event of accident or sickness
- critical illness insurance could repay your mortgage, but it could also buy you a lot of choices
- life insurance – if you weren't here anymore, how would your family keep up with mortgage payments and maintain their standard of living?

PART 2

Criteria

My Story
INTENSIVE RESEARCH

After considering the amount of deposit required and looking at the costs of moving, it all depended on how much we
could borrow.

My first port of call was my existing bank, as we would be
due for an early repayment charge (more on this later) if we
repaid the current mortgage early.

At a time of buying our home together in 2011 interest
rates were on the increase, so I thought it'd be best for us to
go on a five-year fixed interest rate. The downside was that if
we paid that mortgage off before the five years had expired,
we would have a penalty to pay: as we were looking to move
in year four of the five years fixed, the penalty would be a
whopping £10,000. To add fuel to the annoying fire, interest
rates actually did the opposite of what was predicted and
plummeted in 2014, and again in 2016 so I basically missed
out on being able to reduce my monthly payments upon

reviews. Hey-ho – a five-year fixed-term mortgage was the right decision at the time.

My existing lender said they'd use my salary and dividends, so I got the figures from my accountant and gave them what they required: tax calculations (i.e., the self-employed person's version of a P60), bank statements, and company accounts. At this time, my wife was a sole trader and we also had a partnership business, so we had four income streams.

The lender scrutinised the bank statements and picked on every little detail, leaving no stone unturned: 'Why is this payment going out? Why is this one not consistent? What are you paying money to this person for? How much do you spend on food, milk, holidays, kids' clothes etc.?'

After two tiring and annoying weeks, they came back and told us they wouldn't lend us any more than our existing mortgage, even though the new mortgage payment was going to be almost the same as I had already been paying for four years. I felt sorry for the bank mortgage adviser. He was doing his best, but the underwriter said 'no'.

So, what was the problem? My salary and dividends didn't show enough earnings. That year I'd left money in the business because I didn't need it to live on and I didn't want to pay unnecessary tax. At the time, most of my mortgage clients were employed, so my experience in the self-employed market was limited. It's so much easier to place an employed mortgage case, but I wasn't going to let anyone stop me. Gary was on a mission.

I set about researching every single bank and its processes, and how they would view my circumstances, which involved using my mortgage sourcing system. I did reach a point where

I'd found myself a pretty good option. However, I was so far down the road that I thought I might as well continue and speak to the whole market.

All this research took two, solid ten-hour days sitting at a computer, speaking to lenders. That didn't include the countless hours I was stuck on hold, waiting to speak to someone, either!

Almost everybody I spoke to said that, in line with their criteria, they'd want to use salary and dividends. They'd want to average these out over the last two or three years. If salary and dividends are lower in your previous year than in your current year, using an average is going to bring down how much you can borrow.

Throughout my research, I learned that not only did I want a lender who would take into account a higher amount of profit retained in the business, but I also wanted someone who'd consider only my latest year – as a growing business, higher figures mean a larger mortgage. This is the case for a lot of the business owners I work with. I help more people with growing businesses than anyone else. We work with mortgage lenders who use the latest year's income rather than the ones that average out across several years purely because business owners seem to want to borrow more.

Chapter 3
MEETING THE CRITERIA

Once you've done your affordability homework, the next hurdle is the mortgage lender. Every lender has different criteria and will likely come up with different amounts that you can borrow, and the chances of getting a mortgage offer can vary tremendously.

In my honest opinion, you don't need to understand the criteria – unless you've got plans to become a mortgage adviser in the future. I have outlined what I feel are the 'must know' elements to make sure you're prepared for success, whether you're a first-time buyer or moving home, but a specialist adviser could help remove the stress and time finding the right one.

Let's delve into some of the key areas. You may see a heading and think it's not relevant, but I would give the paragraphs a quick read, because understanding the full picture can certainly help you, and you may find that the content is relevant, or it may give you a new line of enquiry to consider.

The more criteria you fit, the greater the number of lenders available to you and therefore the greater your chances of lower interest rates and overall success.

All lenders have different criteria, it's my job to know where you fit best with a lender.

Status of your mortgage application

Self-certification

The removal of self-certified mortgages in 2014 means your income must always be proven. I still feel they have a place in today's market, but I'm unsure whether we'll see them making a return.

Self-certified mortgages required no proof of income: applicants generally signed a waiver to state they could afford the mortgage without having to show any evidence of income at all. This was supposedly a contributing factor in the 2008 credit crunch, as people couldn't keep up with their mortgage repayments.

If you have previously had a self-certified mortgage you're in for a shock. The application process is going to be more frustrating, because lenders continually request more documents or justifications. Even though you may think you have already provided enough, you have to do as asked or you will not get your offer, so listen to the with the advice of a mortgage adviser.

Single or joint application

Mortgage applications can be made individually or by a group of two to four people. When a single person applies for a mortgage, the amount that can be borrowed is assessed on the basis of a single income. To increase your borrowing power, you can apply with a friend, partner or relative.

I wouldn't have been able to get my last two mortgages without Ayesha's income – trying to do it alone it can be a real struggle with house prices.

If you are buying a property with a friend, you may wish to consider your 'exit strategy', that is, agreeing between you exactly what the future looks like and how long you are willing to own the home together.

It is also worth considering the worst case scenario: if you fell out, would the plan be for both of you to sell the property, or would one of you be prepared to buy out the other? Deciding this in advance can help to prevent problems in the future.

Applying as a sole trader

As a sole trader, you've got to take the brave step of working for yourself, throwing caution to the wind. When it comes to your mortgage application, you will need to have been trading for a full twelve months and there's only a small number of lenders who'll consider one year's worth of trading.

If you've got two or more years trading to show, it's a whole new ball game, and the number of mortgage lenders available to you increases significantly. Once you have your second year of trading, you will find mortgage lenders looking to average your income. Most will want to average your last two years' income, which, for a growing business, is a pain, because it can result in a much smaller mortgage being offered.

The good news is that I know first-hand that a small number of lenders can will , assess your ability to keep the business levels up and the money coming in on your latest year's income only. The advantage is of this is that you could get a much larger mortgage. I haven't confirmed which lenders because that could have changed, so speak to an adviser.

We wouldn't have been able to move in 2015 without lenders like these to assess our income.

The key to getting a lender to assess you on the basis of the latest year only is presentation. The right presentation can help them to understanding your business and the reasons for an increase in profits in the latest year. Going over and above supplying the basic documents by providing reports, company or accountant explanations, and management accounts to a lender's underwriter could increase your chances of success, and if you have only been trading for a year, detailing your previous experience in the trade is a great benefit.

When we consider income multiples and averaging your income over 2 years, you'll see just how much this can impact the amount you borrow and therefore the size of house you can buy.

- **Average income example**
  2016 income = £30,000
  2017 income = £40,000
  The average of two years = £35,000

- **Latest year's income example**
  2016 income = £30,000
  2017 income = £40,000
  Income considered by lender = £40,000

It's important you question your adviser to find out if they are using a lender that averages your income or considers latest years especially if affordability is tight.

There are two things to consider when it comes to proving your income. Mortgage lenders like to see a full twelve months' trading; as a sole trader your official tax year runs from 6 April to 5 April each year. As of April 2017, the key documents you need when applying for a mortgage to prove your income as a sole trader are:

- Tax calculation (previously known as an SA302), and
- Tax year overviews

The HMRC will usually issue the Tax calculation and Tax year overview online within forty-eight hours after your tax return submission. They can be requested directly from HMRC and take approximately fourteen days to arrive or you can get them from your accountant. In some instances, an accountant's reference may be acceptable to some lenders which speeds things up.

Example based on one year's accounts.

Let's say you started self-employment in September 2016. If you do not use an accountant, you will submit a tax return to the HMRC between 6 April 2017 and January 2018. That tax return is will cover the period from September 2016 to

April 2017, which is not a full 12 months. The earliest you will become eligible for a mortgage will therefore be April 2018.

But there is an alternative scenario, based on exactly the same dates. If you use a qualified accountant to prepare a full set of twelve months' accounts in September 2017, there may be mortgage lenders who will consider using these figures. This gives you the option to purchase almost eight months sooner.

So bear in mind when you are starting out, if you are using an accountant and you ask them to prepare your tax return in April, if you have plans to buy a home later that year, you should check with them about the twelve months' accounts scenario.

The key figure a mortgage lender is going to want from either your accounts or your Tax calculation is your net profit. Until you've identified this, you will not be able to apply for a mortgage.

(Net profit is the amount left after your expenses have been deducted, and this is the amount you are due to pay tax on.)

If you're sensible and have planned ahead, you can easily get an idea of what your net profit needs to be to achieve your desired mortgage. As I've said, the key to owning your home lies in the preparation.

The tax calculation can also include other sources of income, such as:

- property
- interest
- employment (two or more jobs)
- pensions
- dividends from other companies

The example below is an example of a tax calculation from the HMRC for a limited company director.

Figure 1: Tax calculation

Client Name:	[NAME]		Client Ref:	[REF #]		
Report:	Tax calculation (SA302)		UTR:	[UTR #]		
Assessment Year:	Year to 5 April 2016					
		£	£	£	£

Tax Calculation for Year to 5 April 2016

Income received (before tax taken off)

Pay from all employments		10,599		
Dividends from UK companies (plus 10% tax credits)		38,777		
Total income received			**49,376**	
Less Personal Allowance			(10,600)	
Total income on which tax is due			**38,776**	

Allocation of income to rate bands

Dividend income etc.	31,785.00	@ 10% =	3,178.50
	6,991.00	@ 32.5% =	2,272.07
Total income on which tax has been charged	**38,776.00**		

Income Tax charged	**5,450.57**
Less 10% tax credits on dividends from UK companies (not repayable)	(3,877.60)
Income Tax due after dividend tax credits	**1,572.97**
Tax that you owe	**1,572.97**

Summary

31 January 2017

Balancing payment for tax year to 5 April 2016	1,572.97	
First payment on account for tax year to 5 April 2017	786.48	
Total amount due		2,359.45

31 July 2017

Second payment on account for tax year to 5 April 2017	786.49

Partnerships

A partnership consists of two sole traders working together. Your share of ownership within the partnership will determine the amount of net profit you are due. The lender will use your share of net profit to calculate how much money they will lend you. Everything else is exactly the same as for a sole trader.

Newly self-employed

When you are newly self-employed, it helps to have experience within your trade as an employed person. The question lenders are asking themselves is 'Will this income be able to continue at this level?' So if, for example, you've gone from being an employed electrician to a self-employed electrician, from the lender's point of view, you've got a higher chance of success at being self-employed. However, if you've started a completely new profession when becoming self-employed, for example, electrician to solicitor, they'd assess you as being a higher risk and possibly a lower chance of succeeding in your new business.

Limited companies

If you own 15–20% or more of the shares in your companies, most lenders will classify you as self-employed and you will be assessed on that basis. If you own less than 20%, then lenders will use your pay slips and consider you as employed, which makes things simpler. As I mentioned previously the proportion of shares you will need to own can vary from 15% right up to 33%, depending on the lender.

Most mortgage lenders like you to have been a limited company for a minimum of two years – much like the sole traders and partnerships. You'll need to have a full twelve months' accounts, but in some instances an accountant's reference may be acceptable to some lenders.

The key thing is to find out the timing of your accounts. As an example, my business started on 8 October, but my accounting year runs from 1 April to 31 March. So my first set of accounts wouldn't have been for a full twelve months, and I would have had to wait to apply for a mortgage, similar to the example I provided above.

I see a lot more limited companies whose accounts run for months from the date of incorporation, that is, the date on which they became limited.

> **IMPORTANT TIP:** Make sure your total assets outweigh your total liabilities in your accounts if you want to be considered by the whole of the market.

Almost all lenders will want to know the salary and dividends you have received within a tax year.

Most company directors I speak to, take a basic salary, usually up to the tax threshold and receive dividends. A lot of company directors I speak to will also take a dividend up to the higher-rate tax banding (funds permitting, of course). Your salary and dividends are your personal self-employed 'sole trader' income.

The total is declared on your Tax calculation, as specified above. If you're not drawing dividends, you may not have a

Tax calculation; you may only have pay slips, but don't feel like you're missing out.

Dividends incur their very own tax, which is declared on the Tax calculation. The net figure is what you'll use for the mortgage: add the net dividends to your salary to get the amount for your income multiples to see how much you can borrow.

Changing status halfway through the tax year

Few lenders like applicants going from sole trader to limited company status halfway through the tax year. The most common reasons for changing, from a business owner's perspective, are to get an increase in income, or because turnover and profits are increasing, and/or advice from your accountant.

However, from a lender's point of view, you will not have a full twelve months' accounts as either a sole trader or a limited company, and therefore most will decline an application from someone in this position.

There are some lenders who will consider such an application. However, as with any reduction in the number of lenders under consideration, this generally means an increase in the interest rates available to you, so it could limit your chances of getting the best deal.

Case study: only one year's accounts

Up until June 2013 Joe had been an electrician. Then he had an opportunity to buy a photo booth to earn a bit of money on the side and he took it. Three years later, and he and his wife, Sarah, were working at more than 650 weddings and events over the whole of the UK, with a team of employees and an impressive number of booths.

They wanted a mortgage for a new home for their family, but the problem was, they were self-employed and only had one year's trading accounts to show a prospective lender.

Joe and Sarah were busy running their business and raising two great kids, so they needed someone to find them a mortgage while they focused on their day-to-day lives. Without my help as an experienced mortgage adviser, based on my knowledge as a self-employed business owner, they'd have really struggled to find a lender by themselves.

For most high-street lenders, self-employed workers would need to show two years' accounts. I knew it was possible to get a mortgage with just one year's accounts, but I also knew that the number of lenders is limited and that it comes down to your individual circumstances as well as the deposit you have. Either way, you'll have to jump through many more hoops to get the mortgage you want.

For Joe and Sarah, the lender wanted a full twelve months' trading accounts. Although the business started in June 2013, the first full twelve months' trading accounts weren't available until April 2015. Added to that, they had undertaken a complete job and industry change, which also makes things more risky as there's no previous industry experience, it's not like going from being an employed electrician to working as a self-employed electrician. This can make it even more difficult to be accepted by a lender, as Joe and Sarah found out.

I knew from experience which lenders would be willing to accept Joe and Sarah's application. Once the application was submitted and the documentation obtained, the hard work really began. Active Brokers took care of everything for Joe and Sarah, handling all of the paperwork, liaising with their accountant, chasing solicitors, and updating estate agents at every step of the process. Without this, Joe and Sarah would have found it more difficult to get everything sorted so quickly while running their business and caring for their children.

The mortgage lender took into consideration the company accounts, Tax calculation, and an accountant's reference for the current year. We had the mortgage agreed in no time and they moved in to their new home.

Net profit

For business owners who leave money in the business, you'll be pleased to know there are some sensible lenders out there who'll include your share of net profit in their affordability assessment.

For larger businesses, it's more tax efficient to leave money in your limited company, because the corporation tax rate is lower than the higher-rate personal tax. (Why draw more money from your business, only to pay a higher rate of personal tax, if you don't have to? I get it.)

There are a small number of lenders who'll consider profit retained in a limited company's accounts. This is a considerable advantage for established businesses and can dramatically increase your affordability.

Limited company income calculations

Consider two directors of different companies, one with a 100% shareholding, and the other with 50%.

Net profit after corporation tax = £50,000

Annual salary	=	£11,000
100% shareholder	=	£61,000
50% shareholder	=	£25,000 + £11,000 = £36,000

However, net profits can be considered in a few different ways:

- net profit after tax; or
- net profit before tax, combined with either
  - averaging over two years, or
  - using the latest year

Lenders who take into account net profits will usually add your salary to the profit as well.

If your profit is £50,000 (you may have paid yourself a £40,000 dividend from the profit), and your salary is £11,000, so the figure you can use for income multiples is £61,000.

Tax-efficient limited company director mortgage

As a company director, wouldn't you like to get a mortgage in the most tax efficient way possible? As a sole trader, you only have one option, because mortgage lenders use your net profit before tax to calculate how much you can borrow. But as a limited company director you will find a couple of options available to you:

- Salary + dividends (most high-street banks use this method)
- Net profit + salary

Both have their merits; however, once you earn over £43,001, you become a higher rate tax payer (based on the rate in July 2017)

Let's say, for example, that you own 100% of your business.

- **Option 1**
  You have £80,000 net profit, so you have a corporation tax bill of £16,000.
  You choose to withdraw £64,000 in dividends + your £10,000 salary = £74,000.
  You now have a personal tax bill of roughly £12,175.
  Total tax bill: £16,000 + £12,175 = £28,175.

- **Option 2**
  You have £80,000 net profit, so you have a corporation tax bill of £16,000.
  You choose to withdraw dividends of only £32,000 + £10,000 Salary = £42,000.
  You now have a personal tax bill of roughly £2,025.
  Total Tax Bill £16,000 + £2,025 = £18,025.

As you can see, Option 2 reduces your tax bill by £10,150. My limited company directors love this option because if you do not need to withdraw your dividends, then why would you?

Clearly, using profits to calculate how much you can borrow could increase the size of the mortgage you can get and reduce your tax liability.

Have a look at my blogs and videos for more information about how much you can borrow, and if you want to see how much this approach could benefit you, then please speak to an adviser to discuss your circumstances.

NOTE: Please only use these figures as a rough guide, and remember that lenders have a responsibility to assess whether a mortgage is affordable for you. I am not a qualified accountant and have used online calculators to obtain approximate tax liabilities. Please speak to your accountant to obtain accurate figures based on your personal circumstances.

The following example is a typical set of company accounts provided by an accountant at the tax year end.

Figure 2: Sample profit and loss statement
from a set of company accounts

[COMPANY NAME]

Profit and Loss Account
for the Year Ended 31 March 2015

	Notes	31.3.15 £	31.3.14 £
TURNOVER		443,157	481,422
Cost of sales		187,097	284,076
GROSS PROFIT		256,060	197,346
Administrative expenses		160,007	176,812
OPERATING PROFIT	2	96,053	20,534
Interest receivable and similar income		-	1
		96,053	20,535
Interest payable and similar charges		790	374
PROFIT ON ORDINARY ACTIVITIES BEFORE TAXATION		95,263	20,161
Tax on profit on ordinary activities	3	19,053	4,032
PROFIT FOR THE FINANCIAL YEAR		76,210	16,129

Ratio of assets to liabilities

Assets are the combination of physical items and sums of money you own. This includes:

- cash in the bank
- property
- equipment, plant, etc.

Liabilities are the amounts you owe. This includes:

- bank debt
- money owed to suppliers, contractors, or creditors etc.

If you sold all your assets and paid off your liabilities, what you'd be left with would be the equity.

Your assets need to outweigh your liabilities to the extent that you could pay all your bills and still survive an unexpected outgoing. A healthy business has current assets twice as large as its current liabilities. If your assets are smaller than your liabilities, it's a sign to a mortgage lender that you're potentially struggling.

When reviewing your company balance sheet, you do not want your net assets to be within brackets as this is a negative figure, meaning that your liabilities are greater than your assets.

[COMPANY NAME] (Registered number:)

<u>Balance Sheet</u>
<u>31 March 2015</u>

	Notes	31.3.15 £	£	31.3.14 £	£
FIXED ASSETS					
Tangible assets	5		2,143		2,857
CURRENT ASSETS					
Stocks		113,276		26,044	
Debtors	6	2,700		2,700	
Cash at bank		51,130		95	
		167,106		28,839	
CREDITORS					
Amounts falling due within one year	7	128,823		18,338	
NET CURRENT ASSETS			38,283		10,501
TOTAL ASSETS LESS CURRENT LIABILITIES			40,426		13,358
PROVISIONS FOR LIABILITIES	8		429		571
NET ASSETS			39,997		12,787
CAPITAL AND RESERVES					
Called up share capital	9		100		100
Profit and loss account	10		39,897		12,687
SHAREHOLDERS' FUNDS			39,997		12,787

The company is entitled to exemption from audit under Section 477 of the Companies Act 2006 for the year ended 31 March 2015.

The members have not required the company to obtain an audit of its financial statements for the year ended 31 March 2015 in accordance with Section 476 of the Companies Act 2006.

The director acknowledges his responsibilities for:
(a)   ensuring that the company keeps accounting records which comply with Sections 386 and 387 of the Companies Act 2006 and
(b)   preparing financial statements which give a true and fair view of the state of affairs of the company as at the end of each financial year and of its profit or loss for each financial year in accordance with the requirements of Sections 394 and 395 and which otherwise comply with the requirements of the Companies Act 2006 relating to financial statements, so far as applicable to the company.

The financial statements have been prepared in accordance with the special provisions of Part 15 of the Companies Act 2006 relating to small companies and with the Financial Reporting Standard for Smaller Entities (effective April 2008).

The financial statements were approved by the director on 1 May 2015 and were signed by:

Projections

In some instances, after submitting the application, lenders may ask your accountant to produce projections for the current or next tax year. I recently had an applicant who has only been trading for 1 year, and the lender asked for projections for year 2's trading.

Case study: Self-employed and looking for the biggest mortgage possible

Averaging your income over two or even three years can have a drastic impact on the size of the mortgage you can get.

I recently worked with a professional hairdresser who started his business three years ago. The big issue we faced was his income. He didn't make much in his first year, let's say £10,000, because he had all the set-up costs of buying equipment and renting salon space; although his income was good his expenses were high.

The first year of self-employment is the hardest for a lot of people. You have to learn about self-employment and then go hunting for customers to make a living and cover your monthly bills.

My client's income took a big jump in the third year because of the work and effort he'd put in and the money he'd reinvested into his business over the first two years.

In Year Two, he knew what his clients wanted. He continued to grow his client base and his income increased. With reduced expenses, by the end of the tax year he'd got a decent amount of savings, which allowed him to invest in his own salon. He kitted it out with seriously high-quality professional equipment. These extra expenses brought his income down for Year Two, making it similar to Year One at roughly £10,000.

Year Three began. He was all settled into his own salon and promoting hairstyles for weddings and other special occasions online. His income took another jump, as his expenses were minimal. At the end of Year Three he'd made a decent amount of profit and took an income of £40,000. He came to me asking about mortgages. He'd been to his bank and heard the frustrating words 'we average your income over two years, which meant £40,000 + £10,000 divided by 2 years = £25,000. This would only enable him to borrow £112,500, and with a 10% deposit to find as well, He and his family were getting nowhere.

However, all was not lost, because I knew from my own research in 2015 that there are two mortgage lenders that will consider the latest year's income, providing it can be justified. (This is exactly why I go into the business details of my self-employed client in such depth.)

Using the two lenders who'd consider the latest year's income, I was able to get him close to £180,000 on the income alone. One lender wouldn't take into account child benefit or child tax credit, but the other would. It was a no-brainer who we went with to get the maximum mortgage!

We ended up with a mortgage about £176,000 once they'd factored in the car loan and a couple of small debts, and I'm pleased to say they are now living in their first home.

Other sources of income

Buy-to-let income

If you are renting a property out, almost every lender wants you to have done so for at least a year, and to have declared the income on a Tax calculation under the 'land and property' heading.

However, there's currently small number of lenders who will take rental income into account after only three months, providing it's verifiable on a bank statement.

Multiple incomes

Some lenders will include other sources of income that you may receive. This varies from lender to lender. In some instances, lenders will only include 50% of the amount from these sources, which can represent the difference between your dream home and an average one, or mean having to wait another year, so certainly check the criteria set by the lenders you are approaching.

Having multiple sources of income needn't be a problem with the right lender. I've got multiple sources of income and have many clients who have multiple limited companies, consult as a sole trader, and have a property portfolio.

When you're looking to max out your borrowing, don't forget the following could be considered, depending on the lender:

- child/working family tax credits
- disability allowances
- maintenance, including court-ordered
- foster income
- income derived from lodgers
- income from temporary employment
- income derived from employee benefit trusts (EBTs) or umbrella companies
- income earned in a foreign currency
- rental income (the net figure submitted to HMRC for taxation purposes)
- income from a company the applicant owns that will continue to provide an income into retirement
- investment income
- state pension
- private pension
- company /occupational pension
- widow /widowers' pension
- drawdown on pension fund

You usually need to have been in receipt of the income stream for at least a year, and you need to present the information correctly. Every lender is different so it becomes quite a niche area, and therefore it is the best to seek advice.

Contracting

Contracts are a tricky area and best discussed personally with an adviser. There are so many different sorts of contracts, and IT contractors get special treatment. Below are some lenders' exact criteria, to show you the things to consider when being contracted.

Contractors can potentially be sole traders or limited companies, and this means you're lucky when it comes to mortgages. Lenders will usually consider the daily or monthly rate of the contract, which can hugely increase the amount you can borrow.

Contractors are treated differently from other self-employed people because they have a contract for a set number of days, weeks or months, which guarantees an income. This is why lenders may view them differently.

The key to getting a mortgage with contracts is having a set period for a contract to run for, and a definitive end date. For example, most lenders will want to see a fixed start date and end date, and they will want you, ideally, to have been working on a contract basis for at least six months.

Criteria vary from lender to lender. Here are some key points to consider:

- The contract under consideration for the purposes of a mortgage must be a fixed-term contract; it doesn't matter whether you are employed, a sole trader, a limited company or working under the auspices of an umbrella company.
- You'll need at least one year's experience in the field in which you are contracting, which can be employed experience.
- Some lenders require you to have two years remaining on your contract if you haven't been contracting already for the last 12 months.

- We do have one lender who will consider you after you have been on the contract for six months.
- Copy of latest contract needed as proof.

Daily rates

It's sometimes possible to use your daily rate × 5 × 52 or 48 weeks. You often find that with contracts the current day rate can be higher than is reflected in the previous year's accounts, which can increase the amount you can borrow.

If you have either two years of experience or six months remaining on your current contract, lenders will accept the your daily rate.

> ### Contract example
>
> £550 per day × 5 days × 48 weeks = £132,000 income per year

You could be accepted straightaway, whether you're employed or self-employed, if you have had a one-year contract in the same role previously and you still have twelve months left on it.

Currently on a twelve-month contract: Your current contract must have at least six months remaining on it. If you have less than six months remaining, you must have evidence of a new or renewed contract. Your previous contract must show a term of 12 months of continuous employment. This means there should be no more than two months between contracts.

Currently on a six-month contract: You must have a minimum of three months remaining on your current contract. If you have less than three months remaining, you'll need to show evidence of a new/renewed six-month contract. You'll also need to provide evidence of twenty-four months of continuous employment. This means there should be no more than two months between contracts in the past 24 months.

The lender will also need to see a contract as proof, as well as the last six months' worth of bank statements. This may not apply for longer-term contracts.

Zero-hour contracts: A zero-hour contract means there are no guaranteed hours of work. In April 2017 I made a new discovery: there are a small number of lenders who will consider zero-hour contracts. The main requirement is that you must have been working on such a contract for at least twelve months.

Case study: mortgage success for a self-employed contractors

Active Brokers received a call in June 2016 from a self-employed client who had only two years' accounts. He had one contract that had been running for twelve months, and had gained a new contract from January 2016 that doubled his earnings.

You'll probably be thinking 'Great, it sounds like he could get a mortgage.'

However, his company accounts only showed three months of earnings from the two contracts. The problem he faced was the banks and advisers he'd spoken to would only work off his accounts, which didn't include his second contract.

The client had already had a mortgage of £300,000 agreed in principle by a high-street lender, but the amount he could afford to repay on a monthly basis for his mortgage was far higher than the repayments on £300,000 – plus the cost of his dream house was going to be much higher than £300,000. The idea was to maximise how much he could borrow with a 10% deposit.

I spoke to several lenders and came up against two particular problems in relation to his specific circumstances:

- Contracting to more than one company: most lenders would only consider one contract
- A contract must have been in force for twelve months, and have at least three months left on it.

These requirements were fine for the first contract, but not for the second. I found one lender who would take both contracts into account, providing they had a start date and an end date. This increased the amount my client could borrow from £300,000 to £445,000. With a deposit of £50,000, he could now look at houses priced at £495,000 rather than £350,000.

If you look on www.rightmove.co.uk you can see the difference £150,000 makes to the type of house you can get. Doing this took my client from an average house to his dream home.

Employed

If you're a newly self-employed person with less than two years' full trading accounts, you can strengthen your chances of a positive outcome by applying with an employed applicant. Their salary adds an element of guarantee for the lender.

Here are a few pointers on having your partner's income taken into account if they are employed.

Lenders consider basic salary before tax as the income; if your partner starts to earn overtime, commission and bonuses most lenders will only take into account 50% of these elements of their income.

The longer they are in receipt of these extras the better. A letter from employers can help to persuade some lenders to consider 100% of these amounts, but they take these decisions on a case-by-case basis. So, check your pay slips and speak to an adviser if you want to maximise your mortgage borrowing power.

If you are paying in to a company pension scheme, share scheme, insurance or any other scheme offered by your employer, these are generally seen as an expense and could reduce the amount you can borrow. This is only applicable if they show on your payslips.

Employing your partner

One thing I've seen a considerable increase in recently is limited company business owners or sole traders who want to employ their partners. You need to be aware when you apply for a mortgage that most high-street lenders will want your partner to have been employed by the business for at least three months, depending on the salary.

I've got a client who's started employing his wife as HR manager and paying her a considerable income. The lender declined his mortgage application as they wanted his partner to have been employed for at least six months, whereas she had only been employed for three. (I went to another lender who accepted the three months' salary, but if you are paying a big salary, lenders may want to see that it is sustainable.).

A lender will want will to see three months' to six months' pay slips showing the income declared, and the matching bank statements, with the net amount of salary going into that bank account.

Income multipliers

The old method of working out how much you could borrow was to take your income and use a multiplier. You multiplied your income by the number given, which would give you the maximum you could borrow.

Lenders have a responsibility to assess your income and expenditure to calculate how much you can borrow.

Nevertheless, income multipliers still have a part to play and you can use them to estimate how near or far you are from making your property purchase or move a reality.

Calculating income multiples for single and joint applicants

First-time buyers
Multiply your single or joint income by 4 and 4.49 respectively.

Home-movers
Multiply your single or joint income by 4.49 and 5 respectively.

Although I am finding 5× income is being offered less and less at the present time.

Note: These figures are assuming a mortgage term between 20–35 years. If you are considering less than 20 years then you should reduce the multiplier further i.e. multiple by 3–4.49.

Single income example
£75,000 × 4 = £300,000
£75,000 × 4.49 = £336,750.

This is the range you should be looking in.

Joint income (2 people added together) example
£125,000 × 4.49 = £561,250
£125,000 × 5 = £625,000.

A first-time buyer might not be able to get a mortgage of five times their income, so you should seek advice from an adviser if you do need this.

Income multiples is a very simple method and it omits

many factors, such as any payments you are committed to making, or receive regularly:

- credit cards
- loans
- fares
- pensions
- student loans
- maintenance payments

How much you can borrow massively differs from lender to lender. They all have their own methods and calculations when assessing your affordability, so there's no 'one size fits all'.

Lenders have a responsibility to assess your income and expenditure. Having debts that will remain after completion could reduce the amount you can you borrow.

How lenders differ

Based on a joint annual income of £90,000, the following lenders would calculate affordability as:

Santander	£412,000
Leeds Building Society	£744,678
Platform	£830,630
Skipton	£590,750

(Correct as of 08.07.2017)

Case study: shopping around for the right deal

A client came to me after being turned down by two other high-street lenders because of to their circumstances. He'd been searching online for someone who specialised in arranging mortgages for self-employed people.

The main problem he and his partner faced was that they had not drawn an income from the business, and most lenders didn't take profit into account. To get their dream home, they needed a lender who'd base their calculations on the large amount of retained profit they had in their two limited companies.

After some extensive research, I submitted the application to a lender appropriate to their circumstances. I managed to do in twenty-four hours what it would usually take five to ten days to do. I got my clients agreement in principle for £1.5 million and we began the process to get the mortgage offer as quickly as possible!

Right now, these clients are relaxing in their dream home: a luxury five-bedroom £2 million property!

Summary

As self-certification mortgages are no longer available, you have to be able to provide proof of your income and evidence that the mortgage you are applying for is affordable. Sole traders will need to know their net profit and limited company directors cannot be considered as self-employed unless they own more than 20% of their company. The assets of a limited company will need to exceed its liabilities. You will need to have the following figures at your fingertips:

- gross profit before tax
- net profit after tax
- salary
- dividends

Timing is very important. Most lenders need to see two years' accounts, but if only one year's accounts are available, proof of experience in the trade could help.

Beware of changing status from sole trader to limited company in the middle of a tax year, as it could limit the number of lenders available to you. Projections for income to the year end may be accepted by some lenders.

Other ways to make a persuasive case with the evidence of your income and increasing the amount you can borrow include making an Excel spreadsheet of the income from your property portfolio and having your contractor daily rate taken into consideration. If you are employing your partner, you will need to have a minimum of three months' payslips and bank statements available, and some lenders will require proof of six months' employment.

Income multiples provide a very rough guide to how much you are likely to be able to borrow:

- First-time buyers: multiply your single or joint income by 4 and 4.49 respectively.
- Home-movers: multiply your single or joint income by 4.49 and 5 respectively.

Factors that could reduce the amount you can borrow include any debts that will remain after the completion of the house purchase, but loans in your name that are being repaid by your business could be excluded from consideration by some lenders if than you supply them with an accountant's letter explain the position.

Remember, no two lenders are the same: they don't have the same criteria, and there is wide variation in the amounts they are prepared to lend.

To download the ACTIVE quick reference guide visit: www.activebrokers.co.uk/book

Chapter 4
CREDIT

Credit history

If you have had financial difficulty and are looking for a way onto the property ladder, to move home or looking for a better mortgage deal, having a bad credit history can really feel like a kick in the teeth when it comes to applying for a mortgage.

The high-street lenders' criteria can be strict and generally do prefer you to have a good credit history/score, but of course there are all sorts of reasons that can lead to blemishes on a credit file. It might be the loss of employment or a breakdown in a relationship that have led to the initial problem.

Generally people with poor credit ratings have fewer options, however, all is not lost, because there are many lenders off the high street and smaller building societies that can help you.

Make sure you're on the electoral roll

Check you're registered on the electoral roll at the correct address, it can help your application with a number of lenders. You can register online at any time at www.gov.uk/register-to -vote. Your electoral roll details appear on your credit score, so it's important you're registered correctly. Be aware that your credit score might not be updated overnight, so don't leave it to the last minute. Allow plenty of time for any changes to be made, roughly 8 weeks.

Why is credit score important?

Before agreeing to most forms of credit in the UK, a lender will check with a credit referencing agency to understand

- what credit you have
- how it has been maintained, and
- whether it would be wise to lend to you

Checking your score

Generally, the higher your credit score the better. When checking your rating on credit score websites, remember that lenders have their own 'computer says yes/no' criteria when assessing a mortgage and some lenders are more flexible than others.

Credit score websites

Each website allows you to download your report, which details as a minimum

- your address
- your bank accounts
- any loans, and
- your credit cards

You can get a copy of your report from one of these websites:

- www.experian.com (my top recommendation)
- www.equifax.com (my second recommendation)
- www.noddle.com (free)

If you're not sure what to do, your adviser can guide you through the process of obtaining your report.

When you obtain your credit report, have a look for any mistakes, such as misspelt names, wrong addresses, and any other simple errors. If there are any mistakes, you can apply to have them removed/corrected.

> **TIP:** If you have been turned down for a mortgage, don't despair. Together, you and your adviser can unravel your problems, review your credit report and decide on the best plan of action.

What could harm your credit score?

Excessive applying for credit

If you apply for credit too often in a short space of time, it can harm your ratings and mean the difference between acceptance and refusal.

However, you may still have options. As I have mentioned,

there are lenders 'off the high street', where interest rates might be higher and larger deposits may be required. This is where advice from an adviser can be helpful.

I feel it is important to get the application right first time when applying for a mortgage, so to buy minimise the number of changes you make you your credit arrangements in the lead-up to the time when you wish to buy.

Case study: changing credit cards

I recently had a client with a score of 995 on Experian. He went searching for a property, which took roughly four months. During that time, the agreement in principle that he had expired (it is usually only valid for 30 days), so by the time he found his property we had to reapply for a new agreement in principle.

During the four months he transferred the balance of two credit cards on to new 0% cards and did not cancel the old ones. This transaction reduced his credit score to 750, and as a result he did receive a new agreement in principle from the same lender.

As a result, he was limited in the number of lenders he could apply to. Because he had failed to get an agreement in principle, I had to use a new lender who set a higher interest rate, and required a 15% deposit rather than a 10% deposit. Luckily, he was able to meet the new criteria and he now lives with his family in his dream home.

Missed payments

Missing a payment is a cause for concern for all mortgage lenders. This is because they worry that you will not be able to pay back your mortgage. Keep your payments up to date and make use of a direct debit that goes out soon after your income is credited so you don't have to remember to make the payment.

Defaults and county court judgements

If you miss more than three payments on any form of credit, you're issued with a default. A default can become a county court judgment (CCJ) if you're summoned to court for having not settled the default in advance. Acceptance of a mortgage application will depend on:

- the default amount
- when it was registered, and
- when it was repaid

Dates are really important in this context, and are one of the reasons your adviser needs to see your credit report.

Involuntary arrangements

An involuntary arrangement is an agreement with your creditors to pay all or part of your debts. You agree to make regular payments to an insolvency practitioner, who will divide this money between your creditors. Your mortgage application is considered on a case-by-case basis, so speak to an adviser about your circumstances if you currently have an involuntary agreement with your creditors. I have only found lenders who will consider your application once you have been discharged from such an agreement for a minimum of twelve months.

Bankruptcy

Mortgage applications are considered on a case-by-case basis, so speak to an adviser about your circumstances. In my experience, lenders who will consider your application once you have been discharged from bankruptcy for a minimum of three years

What bad credit means for your mortgage

If you've had credit problems you may have been rejected by a high-street lender. However, there are specialist lenders that cater for borrowers with a chequered credit history.

If there are any major problems with your credit rating such as missed payments, defaults or county court judgements etc., remember that time is a great healer and most credit problems eventually drop off your credit report in six years from when the problem was last noted on your credit report.

In my experience, it might be possible to obtain a mortgage as early as three months after the bad credit has been registered. As it depends on the amount it is very difficult to specify the exact criteria.

If you have had problems with credit recently, the best

thing is to get in touch with an adviser with your credit report to hand. It's worth noting the following points:

- the majority of missed payments, defaults and CCJs can be ignored after they have been satisfied/settled for two years.
- a minimum deposit of 15% is required if you have had missed payments, defaults and CCJs.

Improving your credit score

There are a couple of reason clients get declined:

- lacking a positive track record because they've not needed to use credit facilities in the past (first time buyers); and
- getting credit but maintaining it badly (not paying or paying late).

If you have a credit card, spending on it regularly, and repaying it shows a mortgage lender you can manage money. But be aware that all forms of credit come with interest rates, and you need to look at these very carefully when choosing credit.

Luckily, there are a few things you can do to get your credit score in shape, and even if you can't get it to perfection, there are still some options to help you get a mortgage:

Note: I cannot provide advice on unsecured lending.

1. **Take a good look at your credit report:** It sounds simple, but don't just assume your credit score is fine. Make sure you know what you're dealing with. Look closely to see if there are

any mistakes you could challenge them on to help improve your score. When you challenge a mistake on your credit report, the credit reference agency have up to twenty-eight days to remove it, or to justify why it's staying on your report.

2. **Plan and manage for the long term:** Improving your credit rating in the long term means demonstrating that you can handle borrowed money responsibly, and that takes time. You can't fix everything in a few months. The best thing you can do is start planning in advance to make sure your credit score is in good shape. Begin as early as you can to help things runs smoothly.

To improve your score in the long term

- pay all your debts on time, or early if possible
- use your credit card responsibly, to show you can handle debt, and
- make sure you know exactly what you're getting into when you take on credit by checking the limits and the interest rates

3. **Don't take on more debt:** It could be a bad idea to take on more debt or risk until your mortgage is sorted out. It's even better if you can avoid debt altogether (apart from a well-managed credit card to demonstrate your creditworthiness). Make sure you cancel anything you're no longer using, like unused credit cards.

4. **Take a break:** If you've been refused a mortgage recently, or had multiple credit checks, it could be better for you to hold off for a while. Too many checks in a short period of time can deter lenders – it shows that either you're looking to apply

for more credit, or other lenders have checked your credit score and made the decision not to finance you. I usually recommend no more than three checks in a six-month period.

Summary

Make sure you are equipped with the basics by downloading your credit report from Experian, Equifax, or Noddle. You also need to check that you are on the electoral roll and apply at the earliest opportunity if you are not.

To protect your credit score, avoid applying for credit in the three to six months leading up to your mortgage application. Once the application has started, do not apply for credit until you have completed and moved into the new property. Follow the advice given by credit reference agencies to improve your credit score.

Any debt problems you have had do not necessarily mean that you will never be able to get a mortgage, simply that you may have to wait a bit longer:

- defaults and CCJs over two years old may be ignored
- you may need to have been discharged from an involuntary arrangement for twelve months before applying for an audience
- you may need to have been discharged from bankruptcy for three years before applying for a mortgage
- Speak to an adviser about your credit report.

To download the ACTIVE quick reference guide visit: www .activebrokers.co.uk/book

PART 3

Terms

My Story
THE MOST SUITABLE DEAL

Bearing in mind affordability and criteria, I had to consider what mortgage terms I would be offered.

My mortgage lender took into account my company's net profit, plus my salary from the last year's company accounts. These were considered alongside Ayesha's sole trader net profit, which meant we could double our mortgage. Amazing what you learn from a bit of research!

But being able to almost double our mortgage was certainly going to double our monthly mortgage payment! Having had a mortgage for nine years, we'd reduced our mortgage term from twenty-five years to sixteen years. I knew that, as I was only thirty-four, extending the term was a good option. I looked to increase it to age seventy. Although I'm planning to never really retire, this was the maximum term available to me without affecting the amount I could borrow. This pushed the mortgage term up to thirty-five years, and reduced the monthly mortgage payment to what I'd been paying for the last four years. There was no doubt it was affordable.

However, increasing the term of a mortgage massively increases the amount of interest you pay.

My view is that as business continues to improve, I can reassess the mortgage term and/or make overpayments to reduce the balance more quickly, thus reducing the amount of interest I pay. I don't intend to have the mortgage for the full thirty-five years, and my plan is to put as much income as possible into it so I can repay it quicker.

I'm someone who likes a bit of security and knowing what I've got to pay each month so I can budget. I didn't want to have the worry that my mortgage payment might change so I chose a fixed-rate mortgage. I reviewed two- and five-year fixed-rate mortgages to see which interest rate I preferred. The monthly payments for the two-year fixed-rate mortgage was very similar to what I was already paying, whereas the extra security of the five-year one pushed the payment up a fair bit.

I didn't want any errors when applying so I made sure the terms fitted the criteria. Any error in my assessment or calculations would have meant we wouldn't get the mortgage.

At this point, every bit of due diligence and planning had been done and it was time to submit a request for an agreement in principle to the mortgage lender. This involved putting all the information I'd collated into their online system.

The application was submitted by one of my advisers, and after twenty-four long hours the case was reviewed by the underwriter, who provided an initial acceptance of our case. The first important step was complete a successful agreement in principle.

Chapter 5
TYPES OF MORTGAGE

I'm now going tell you about the options available for your new mortgage. There are many bells and whistles, not all of which will apply to you. We all have unique circumstances – especially the self-employed – so an adviser will discuss these with you.

Interest rates are one of the main considerations when looking for a mortgage. The lower the interest rate, the less you'll pay each month.

For many self-employed people, it can be difficult to navigate the mortgage minefield and decide whether to get a commercial or a residential mortgage. Home and work life can often be very much the same thing, which blurs the divide that employed people often enjoy.

I have spoken with many business owners who have bought premises for their growing company and rent their residential home. Bear in mind that if you work from home there are considerations for a mortgage lender based on the percentage of your home you use for business purposes.

When considering what type of mortgage you need, ask yourself the following questions: do you live here? Is there a bedroom, a bathroom, a kitchen, a garden and all the other things you'd find in a home? If so, it's a residential mortgage that you need – even if you work here in a study, or work from home.

Is the place just for work? Are there offices or stock or machinery stored here? If the property's main purpose is for your business, then you need a commercial mortgage.

Is your property literally half and half? I don't just mean a study (that would need a residential mortgage). If, for example, the property in question is a pub with a living area for the landlords attached, you need a semi-commercial mortgage. These are very specialist arrangements and not something you can just search for by yourself.

The process can be time-consuming and especially frustrating when you have a million-and-one other things on your to-do list. You're confused and anxious to get the right mortgage, and without advice you could waste huge amounts of time and energy without achieving anything, so speak to an adviser about your circumstances.

Residential mortgages

Your home is the place you live, sleep and eat. Even if you work here in a study or have a space just for your self-employed career, primarily it's still a home and therefore requires a residential mortgage. Generally, residential mortgages can last up to around thirty-five years, but with a few lenders it could be possible to run for longer. Many clients I have dealt with aim to repay their mortgage by the time they retire, so they can reduce their outgoings once they stop working full time.

An important difference between commercial and residential mortgages is that the residential mortgage market is regulated, whereas the commercial market isn't. This suggests that buying a property with a commercial mortgage is based on the performance of your business, and should therefore be a more straightforward and logical process – however, this does depend on the merits of each individual case.

Commercial mortgages

Commercial mortgages can be taken out for offices, warehouses, and any place where the sole purpose of the property is for work. If you don't intend to run your business from the property, it's not a commercial mortgage that you need.

- I get a lot of clients who want to buy commercial property, usually for one of the following reasons: They are buying a commercial property to occupy, that is, to work in and run their business from.
- They are buying the commercial property for investment purposes, to be rented out.
- They are buying business premises and the business that is trading in them

When you're self-employed and your business world merges

into your home life, how do you know that you're still getting the best of both worlds when it comes to a mortgage?

As with any mortgage, you need to show that the business occupying the building can afford the repayments and can pass the usual borrower affordability tests.

Typically, commercial mortgages can last from one year up to fifteen years – which is a lot shorter than residential mortgages. While a shorter repayment period may seem great, be aware that you'll usually need a minimum 30% deposit in the first place.

Lenders will look at your current lease payments and your business performance as a whole when working out what you can afford. However, this does have its downsides. If you're a first-time commercial mortgage buyer, for example, rates will be typically higher, at roughly 8% (real rates will depend on your specific circumstances, so do get in touch if you would like a personalised quote). This is because there's more risk for the lender. They need to know that your business will be a success and you'll be able to keep paying the mortgage.

After twelve to twenty-four months of your commercial mortgage have passed, you may have the option of reviewing your loan. By then, you'll be classified as an 'experienced commercial mortgage owner' by the lenders, and more favorable rates may be available to you.

Bridging finance

A bridging loan is something that's usually taken out over twelve or twenty-four months. It's raised for any number of purposes and the interest can be added on to the property. It just makes it easier to borrow quickly. Bridging finance can be arranged in anything from two to four weeks. Most mortgage lenders want to see a repayment strategy, such as a property that you're selling, but you need to borrow money for the short term to secure the property you want to buy.

Be aware that the interest rates on this type of mortgage are much, much higher than for other types of mortgage.

Mortgage term

The length of your mortgage is determined by how much you can afford to pay each month and the income you've got left after paying all your monthly expenses. Mortgage terms generally run from 5 to 35 years with most lenders, and many will allow you to have them until age seventy without too many difficulties. With a mortgage that would take you up to age 85 (the maximum available) you generally have to prove that you have enough pension or property income to continue to afford the monthly mortgage payment.

It's best to choose the shortest term possible within your affordability, as this reduces the total amount of interest you pay over the length of the mortgage.

Paying off your mortgage

Lenders will often let you personalise your mortgage, and when they recommend a mortgage, all advisers should provide you with a European Standardised Information Sheet (ESIS) or Key Facts Illustration – I call this a quote. It provides a full outline of the mortgage to be applied for, including all the terms and conditions, fees and charges.

There are two main ways to repay your mortgage.

Repayment

Repayment is the preferred method of repaying your mortgage. It means that you pay off both the capital and the interest every month, so that by the end of your mortgage term, the whole amount will have been paid off.

Interest only

Interest-only mortgages are now more relevant for buy-to-let properties used for investment purposes. It is assumed that you intend to repay the mortgage from the sale of the property or other investments.

Caution: For years, interest-only mortgages were very easy to get, but now lenders have made it very difficult to obtain an interest-only mortgage on the house you intend to live in, by requiring high minimum deposit or equity amounts and high minimum incomes.

If you need an interest-only mortgage or assistance, it is best to speak to an adviser.

Figure 3: Capital owed under interest-only and repayment mortgages

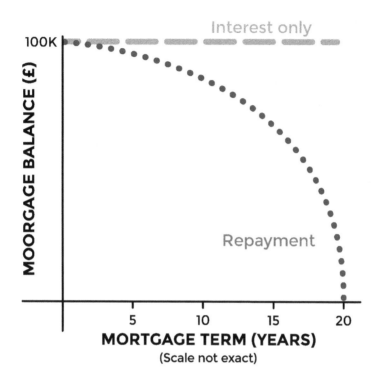

Interest rates

Interest rates are constantly changing, as is the relationship between them and the interest rate lenders are charging you.

Bank of England base rate

The Bank of England base rate is reviewed every month and impacts on the interest rates available from banks and what is available to you.

Standard variable rate

Mortgage lenders have their own standard variable rates. These are much higher than the Bank of England base rate, and they dictates all the deals that are available to you.

You're most likely to go onto the standard variable rate after fixed, tracker or discounted deals (see below) have finished. The standard variable rate tends to be around 4–5% and therefore much more expensive.

(At one point in the 1980s the standard variable rate was up as high as 15%. My parents are always talking about this.)

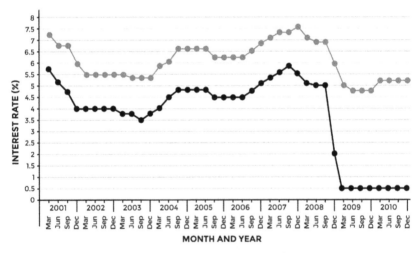

Figure 4: Alignment between Bank of England base rate and standard variable mortgage rates

Standard Variable Rate (SVR) of Hanley Economic Building Society over the past 10 years
Bank of England Base Rate over the past 10 years

Fixed interest rate

This means you can keep your monthly mortgage payment the same for a certain period, so you'll know exactly how much you need to pay each month. Once the fixed period has ended, you are likely to go on to the standard variable rate.

Fixed rates are generally available for two, three, and five years, though some lenders currently offer ten years.

Figure 5: Comparison between fixed and variable mortgage rates

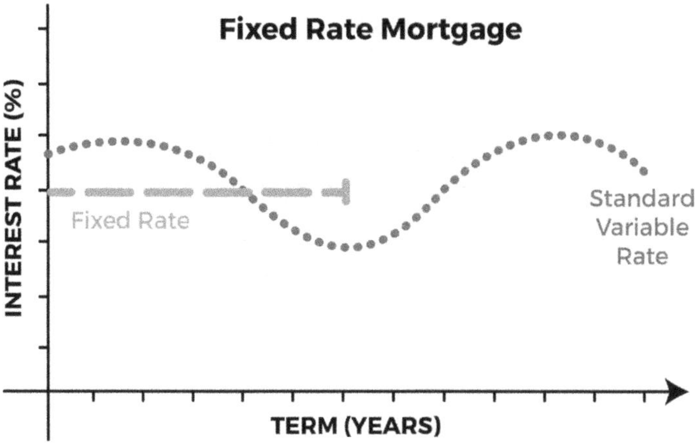

Fixed Rate Mortgage / INTEREST RATE (%) / Fixed Rate / Standard Variable Rate / TERM (YEARS)

Tracker interest rates

With a tracker mortgage, your repayments will fluctuate in line with the Bank of England (BoE) base rate.

For example, the Bank of England base rate is currently 0.25%. If your tracker mortgage rate is 1%, you'll be paying 1.25%. This means if the base rate increased to 1.5%, you would pay 2.75%; if the base rate reduced to 0% you'd be paying 1%.

Over the last five to six years, with interest rates being

so low, there hasn't been that much difference between the percentages of tracker and fixed rates.

You usually get some extra flexibility with tracker rates, through options such as

- no early repayment charges
- unlimited over payments, and
- offset facilities.

I'll explain all these benefits later.

A tracker rate normally lasts for two years, after which you usually revert to standard variable rate. There are lenders who offer lifetime trackers, which continue for the full term of the mortgage.

Figure 6: Alignment between tracker interest rates and Bank of England base rate

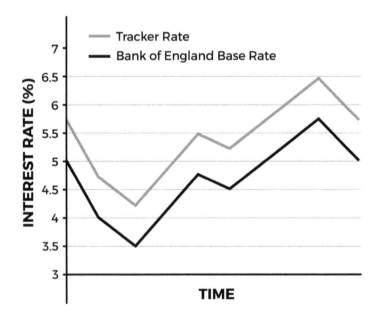

Discounted

With a discounted mortgage, you get a discount off the standard variable rate. If the standard variable is, say, 5%, the mortgage lender will give you a 1% discount for two years, so your payment will be based on 4%.

As with a tracker you need to bear in mind that if the lender decides to increase their standard variable rate, your payment is will increase too.

Figure 7: Comparison between discounted mortgage rate and standard variable mortgage rate

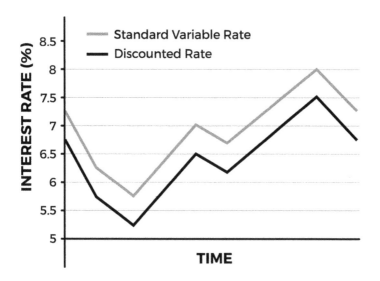

Offset

An offset mortgage can be any of the types explained above that also allows you to link your mortgage to a savings or current account. The benefit of doing so is that by 'offsetting' your savings you're reducing the interest charged. Advisers generally recommend you keep your offset amount above 10% of the mortgage balance to get real benefit, but if you have a substantial monthly income or credit to a current account this can also be beneficial.

This is how it works. If your mortgage balance is £300,000 and you have £30,000 in a linked current or savings account which is being offset, the mortgage lender only calculates the interest you pay you based on £270,000 instead of the full £300,000. The interest from the £30,000 you're saving can be used either to reduce your monthly mortgage payment or to reduce the term of the mortgage.

When you've got a large amount of spare cash, rather than paying a lump sum towards your mortgage and losing access to your money (as it becomes 'tied up in the house'), you can still access it immediately by withdrawing some from your offset amount.

Figure 8: Mechanism of offset mortgages

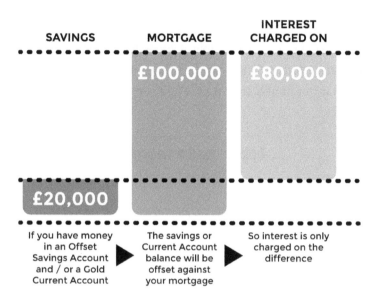

Overpayments

As I mentioned earlier, my main focus to reduce the interest I pay and reduce my mortgage term. With most mortgage interest rate deals, lenders limit you to 10% of the starting year balance. When the deal comes to an end, you're free to overpay as much or as little as you like, and this is also the time to review your mortgage (more on this later).

Most mortgages lenders operate a daily rate of interest, so if you overpay £100 today, you will no longer be paying interest on that £100 tomorrow.

Something to consider is if you want to pay off more than 10% is that you could be in line for an early repayment charge (see below).

If you have a large lump sum of money coming to you (a bonus or an inheritance, perhaps) and you're thinking of making an overpayment, you need to consider how long your 'deal' period is for. For example, if you will receive your lump sum while you are in the middle of a five-year fixed-rate deal, you may not be able to make the large overpayment without penalty.

Figure 9: Impact of overpayments

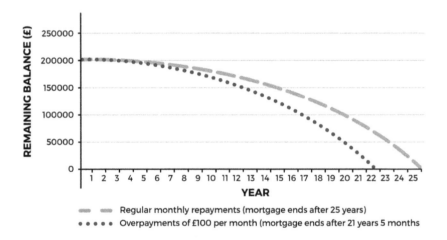

Early repayment charges

The mortgage lender agrees to give you a better rate for a period of time in exchange for committing to them for a number of years. If you repay the mortgage during the deal period, whether it's a fixed, tracker or discounted mortgage, there may be a penalty to pay them.

Early repayment charge example

An early repayment charge applies if you want to repay the mortgage early.

The charge in this example is calculated using a loan amount of £425,000.00 and is based on:

- 2% of the outstanding loan if the mortgage is repaid before 31 July 2018
- 1% of the outstanding loan if the mortgage is repaid before 31 July 2019

Based on the original amount borrowed, the early repayment charges that could apply would be:

- £8,590.00 if the mortgage is repaid before 31/07/2018.
- £4,340.00 if the mortgage is repaid before 31/07/2019.

Early repayment charges vary depending on the product and they could be as high as 5% throughout every year of your deal, so please check with your adviser.

When you repay a mortgage there may also be some other administration fees payable to the lender, so please check the Key Facts Illustration or ESIS for the full terms of early repayment.

Valuations

Let me emphasise that I am not a surveyor, and mortgage advisers are not allowed to recommend which type of valuation is suitable for your property. My aim is to provide information to help you decide.

Standard mortgage valuation reports

A standard mortgage valuation report is a report based on a physical inspection of a property carried out by a chartered surveyor on behalf of your lender, to ensure that the value of the asset for which they are providing the finance is high enough to secure the loan.

For example, if you want to borrow £200,000 on top of a £40,000 deposit to buy a house with a total purchase price of £240,000 but the mortgage valuation suggests the property is only worth £220,000, mortgages lenders will only base their offer on their valuation. What this means at this stage is that you either renegotiate the purchase price or make up the shortfall, i.e. £20,000 in this example.

The important thing to remember is that this standard valuation may tell the lender what they need to know, but it won't consider any potential future structural problems or costs that the property could represent. Furthermore, some lenders won't show you the report at all unless you ask to see it – even though you may have paid for it!

The lender uses this to get an independent assessment of the property that they can trust. A surveyor will visit your property, have a look around, do some research on the general condition and valuations of properties in the area. The standard mortgage valuation report is then compiled for the lender.

If you're lucky, your lender might carry out the valuation for free, as they're legally obliged to do one anyway. Otherwise, fees may vary, but you should be able to find out in advance how much it will cost from your adviser. Most lenders vary their fees according to the value of the property.

The Money Advice Service estimates most valuation fees are from £150 to £1,500 – which could come as quite a shock! Make sure you check with your lender before a survey is conducted and budget for this cost if you need to.

The whole process is a bit different if the property is in Scotland. North of the border, the vendor has to undertake a mortgage valuation before putting the property up for sale. This home report must include a survey by a qualified surveyor, much like in the rest of the UK, but it must also include an energy performance certificate and a completed property questionnaire, to give the buyers all the facts and figures they'll need about the property.

A standard mortgage valuation report is only required if you're borrowing money requiring security against the property – in effect, for a mortgage. Beyond this survey, however, there are several other surveys to consider (see below) that can give you further information on the property you're interested in, reducing the risk of any nasty surprises later on.

All mortgage lenders need the basic valuation, so there's nothing you really need to do about it, but it's good to know what's happening.

Surveys

Getting the right survey done before buying your property is extremely important. Without the right survey on the property, you might think you've found your dream home only to realise later it's riddled with problems.

Most lenders only offer a basic or a homebuyer's survey. If

you want a full structural survey or any more in-depth survey, you may need to find one independently.

Homebuyer's survey report

A homebuyer's survey report is an in-depth survey that's perfect for normal properties that don't appear to be in bad condition. It is the next step up from the mortgage lender's valuation report, so it will give you an idea of the problems the property has without going into too much detail. It's ideal for properties that have been kept in good condition, as it can confirm what major problems the property has, if any.

But bear in mind there's still quite a lot that this report doesn't do. It's a casual report: the surveyor will take a look at the property and point out any glaring problems that need to be fixed immediately. This survey isn't going to look under the floorboards or assess the plumbing and wiring of the property, nor is the surveyor likely to highlight any little issues that could become bigger problems in the future.

As you might expect, the price of a homebuyer's survey is a bit more than that of a valuation report, with prices starting at around £400 on average. But once again, it can vary depending on the surveyor and the value of the property. You might be able to negotiate a discount with your lender or surveyor for both a homebuyer report and a standard mortgage valuation report if you buy them at the same time.

New-build survey

A new-build survey is another kind of basic survey, designed to find the faults most common to newly built houses.

It is often relatively superficial but many home buyers find that with brand new properties anything more comprehensive is unnecessary. The report will consider the general construction of the property. As you might expect with newly built properties, there often has not been enough time for any serious problems such as damp or roof damage to arise, as they might have done in older properties.

The process for this survey is similar to the process for the other surveys. However, once the survey has been completed, the developer of the new-build site should fix the faults highlighted by the report before you move in.

Costs are smaller for this survey than others, as there may be less to document for a new build. Average costs tend to be around £300, depending on the size and location of the property.

Full buildings or structural survey

A full buildings survey, also called a structural survey, is the most intense, in-depth property survey you can commission. It will give you a detailed report on both the current problems with the property and those that could arise in the future, to enable you to budget and prepare yourself.

This type of survey can cost upwards of £600, or it may be calculated on the price of the property. When you consider what emergency repairs to your property could cost, it could be worth paying a little bit extra now to have some warning. In some cases, house buyers have been able to use the findings of a full buildings survey to renegotiate the purchase price of the property, to reflect the cost of the repairs that would be necessary on completion.

Agreement in principle or decision in principle

Once you have been through all the hoops, this is the final piece of the puzzle after getting the affordability, criteria and terms accepted.

Pretty much everything done so far is processed online by your adviser and submitted to the lender for them to do a credit check. This process can take from two to twenty-four hours and depends on the lender.

Make or break

If you don't get this agreement, it could mean going to a new lender, who may well only be offering a higher rate, or it could mean you have to wait because some problem (which should have been identified in the early steps) has been flagged up by the lender.

If the preparation has been done properly and you get an agreement at this stage, the next step is to find a home. On passing the important agreement in principle milestone, you should feel confident about your chances of getting a mortgage.

Summary

First of all you need to consider whether a commercial or residential is most suitable for you, depending on the use the property will be put to. Then you need to consider which type of mortgage is most suitable, bearing in mind the following facts:

- the shorter the term of the mortgage, the less overall interest you will pay
- a repayment mortgage guarantees that your mortgage balance is £0 by the end of the term
- an interest-only mortgage means that your mortgage balance does not reduce. And you will owe the same as at the beginning (lender criteria for these are strict, so it is best to speak to an adviser)
- an offset mortgage allows you to link your mortgage to your current or savings account, limiting the amount of interest you pay

Interest rates broadly reflect the Bank of England base rate, which is reviewed every month. The following options are available:

- the standard variable rate is set by the lender
- with a fixed-rate mortgage, your monthly repayments will stay the same for a number of years
- a tracker rate follows the Bank of England base rate, which means that your monthly repayments could fluctuate
- a discounted rate incorporates a discount offered by the lender on their standard variable rate, which means that your monthly repayments could fluctuate

While you are in a mortgage deal, you may be limited to 10% of the mortgage balance if you want to make extra payments, and you may be liable for penalties if your overpayments go over this limit, or if you repay the mortgage in full before the end of the term.

All mortgages require a valuation to be carried out. These are the different types of valuation available:

- a standard mortgage valuation is for the lender's benefit and is a prerequisite for a mortgage
- a homebuyer's survey is for the buyer's benefit and could offer more protection
- a full structural survey is the most comprehensive survey available

Once you have an agreement in principle from a lender, you are well on the way to getting a mortgage.

Chapter 6
FEES

There are many fees that come with a mortgage, but not all of them are relevant to every application. This is a list of fees you may incur; remember to add these into your budget. Your adviser will be able to tell you whether they are relevant to your application.

Booking fee

This is a fee charged up front by the lender to reserve the interest rate and process the application. It is also be known as an application or reservation fee, and ranges from £99 to £299.

Arrangement fee

The arrangement fee is what you pay the lender to set up your mortgage. This ranges from £0 to £1,999. You have the option with most lenders to add this amount to the mortgage.

A general rule of thumb is the higher the fee, the lower the interest rate offered to you. However, if you have bad credit or need something a little more bespoke, the interest rate and the arrangement fee can be higher than average.

Stamp Duty Land Tax (SDLT)

Buying a property or land over a certain price in England, Wales and Northern Ireland incurs stamp duty. Currently the threshold is £125,000 for residential properties and £150,000 for non-residential land and properties.

This tax no longer applies in Scotland, where, you pay Land and Buildings Transaction Tax instead when you buy a property.

You pay the tax when you:

- buy a freehold property
- buy a new or existing leasehold
- buy a property through a shared ownership scheme, or
- are transferred land or property in exchange for payment, for example, you take on a mortgage or buy a share in a house.

The link I currently use to calculate stamp duty for my clients is https://www.stampdutycalculator.org.uk/

Solicitors' fees

When purchasing a property, you're required to choose your own solicitor to assist with your purchase and pay your stamp duty. This is often the slowest part of the mortgage application process.

Costs vary when choosing a solicitor. I have a great panel of 26, of which I use six or seven regularly. As a rough example, the searches cost approximately £300 upfront and £900 on completion = £1,200 + your stamp duty.

The fee will vary according to whether you are buying a freehold or a leasehold property (there is more information on this in the 'Identify' section of the book), you have a gifted deposit, the property purchase price and other factors, so it is best to get a personalised quote.

If you have a property to sell, you can expect to pay this fee twice, i.e. £1, 200 for each property, making a total of £2,400.

Advisers' fees

Your adviser will discuss their company's fees with you in the initial disclosure session, before any work is undertaken. Advisers are also paid commission from the lender.

Valuation fees

See Chapter 5 for details of the various types of valuation. Valuation fees range from £150 to £1,500.

Moving fees

Moving house has a reputation to be one of the most stressful events you can go through in life, when we moved home in 2015 I spoke to three local removal firms and found two different ways they calculate their fee:

- a day rate, working out the size of van and number of people
- a box rate, depending on the number of boxes needed

There may also be extra fees if you have, say, a large number of books, or high-value items, or items that need specialist packing.

A rough estimate for a four-bedroom house, based on my own move, is £1500.

Estate agents' fees

It often helps to speak to two or three agents locally, to find out what they charge, cost and check out who is likely to be the best for your area based on 'For Sale' or 'Sold' signs.

Local agents in my area who take care of the whole process of selling your home charge roughly between 1–2% of the sale price.

There are now many online agents, such as Purple Bricks and others, who work on a flat fee. They require you to take your own photos of the property and upload them online, and they generally charge a flat advertisement fee of about £500–£1000.

Personally, I prefer to use a 'real' as opposed to a virtual agent because they do majority of the work for you and make sure you get the very best price for your house.

Summary

There are a number of costs associated with buying a property over and above the mortgage repayments. Make sure you don't overlook the following fees:

- booking fee, generally payable on submission of the application to the lender
- arrangement fee: usually payable on application to the lender or on completion, but some allow you to add it to the loan
- Stamp Duty Land Tax (SDLT), payable to HM Revenue and Customs and usually taken care of by your solicitor. It will be included in the amount you pay on completion.
- solicitors usually charge an amount upfront when you instruct them, and the rest is payable on completion
- adviser fees: some brokers or advisers may charge a fee for their services
- valuation fees: the price varies depending on the type of valuation you want
- Moving fees: these are dependent on the volume and the nature of the contents of your home
- Estate agents: online estate may charge less than high-street ones, but in my experience you get what you pay for

PART 4
Identify

My Story
FINDING 'THE ONE'

Finally, we had our agreement in principle: a valued piece of paper that said, 'Yes, you can borrow £x', so we embarked on putting our house on the market. We had three local estate agents come to value the house. I think it's a good idea to pick companies who've got 'for sale' or 'sold' boards up in your area because they understand that area and what the competition is like.

Our house sat on the market, with only three viewings for almost eight weeks. What made it worse was that we'd seen a house we liked and were unable to put in an offer because we hadn't sold our property yet. This is pretty common with a lot of clients I've worked with. The feedback we were getting was that our upstairs space was quite big, but with only three rooms and a toilet the downstairs space was relatively small.

We started to consider the layout of the rooms. We had put a sofa across our large rectangular living room three-quarters of the way down, to create a play space – and so we could hide our daughters' toys behind the sofa and still have a lounge in the evenings! On the other hand, this was making the room appear small. The doors into the garden were also behind the sofa, so it was, in effect, quite an obstruction.

After some much-needed furniture movement, we made the room feel double the size. You could walk into the room and straight out of the back doors into the garden. The girls' toys went up to their bedroom. It really was game changing!

It's an important point: make sure you consider everything about your home when looking to sell. You want to maximise your space and make it easier for potential buyers to see your house in the best light possible. You want buyers to walk in and be able to imagine themselves living there. Paint the walls neutral colours so the buyers can visualise their own colours on there.

> **TIP:** Pastel colours combined with whites can make your room look larger.

When our contract with our current estate agents came to an end, I went back to an estate agent I had used previously and said we'd like to use them. They arranged to come and take some pictures of our home.

By this time the house we'd liked had gone. However, we'd constantly been looking online and another one came up – one we loved.

- It was in the area we wanted
- It was walking distance from the school we wanted

- It had a nice big plain garden for me (I'm not into gardening)
- It had a drive for the cars
- And a playroom for the kids

It was perfect!

We booked a viewing (even though we hadn't sold our house yet). As soon as we walked into the house we knew this was 'the one'! I looked at Ayesha and she felt the same. The girls were with us, and they were running around the garden. It was July, so the garden was in full sun. The place was in immaculate condition.

After only thirty minutes, we made an offer.

We formalised the offer through the estate agents after we left, because they are obliged to tell you if you've been outbid. But we still needed to sell our house.

Our house went back on the market the next day, and two days later we had the horrible call telling us our dream house had been sold to a cash buyer. Damn!

As it turned out, I'd got quite friendly with the guy who was selling the house, as he had started coming to my gym in the mornings. I built a relationship with him and he kept asking if we had had any more viewings. He was slightly older than us, but his children were all under 10 and going to the school we wanted to send our girls to.

Within two weeks we had had another three viewings and a solid offer from a cash buyer. I made a decision. I was going to put an offer on the house anyway. I called the seller of our dream home and offered more than the asking price and more than the other cash buyer. I immediately formalised it through the estate agents.

I was at the solicitor waiting to sign lease papers on new business premises and had to sign lease papers when I got a call: the seller had spoken to his wife and they accepted our offer.

I started dancing round their office – he must have thought I was barking mad!

My father has always said to me 'you don't ask, you don't get' and I live by that in both my personal and business life. I felt sorry for the other couple but, as the sellers explained, they were cash buyers coming from London, so they could buy anything. The sellers could see we would love the house and enjoy it as they had done. As they had invested a lot of time and made many improvements, it was personal for them – and thank goodness.

Chapter 7
THE RIGHT PROPERTY

House prices have been climbing again. With the demand for properties rising and the supply of homes is still not big enough, homes are scarce. Many houses don't stay on the market for long, so when you stumble over a great-looking house, how do you decide whether it's the right property for you before someone else gets their hands on it?

Whether you're searching seriously with a budget in mind, or just having a casual nose around, finding a home isn't always plain sailing. From dodgy surveys to being gazumped, house-hunting can be a heart-wrenching experience. However ugly it might be, it's best to search wisely and uncover any problems early on, to avoid the devastating realisation of finding structural problems and nightmare neighbours once you've moved in!

So here some handy hints to help you make sure you find the right property.

How to choose the perfect property

Property types

When you picture your future home, what do you see? Consider what you really want from the property. Would a mobile home do? Would you be happy squeezed into a terraced property? Or is a detached farmhouse perfect for your family?

It really does depend on your specific circumstances right now, and your future plans. A two-bedroom flat or maisonette might be great for you now, but what about three or seven years down the line? A mortgage is a huge commitment: you'll want to make sure you're getting the right property, even if it is just to get your foot on the property ladder.

When considering the property type that would best suit you, have a look on websites like Rightmove, to see the floor plans and get an idea of what is available and at what price.

You might also want to consider a self-build, where you purchase land and build your home from the foundations up. This is great if you're a bit more adventurous – or too OCD to live in a home that doesn't meet your exact needs. Self-building your property can give you the freedom to make your dream home a reality.

The key information a mortgage adviser needs at the point of application are whether it's:

- a house
- a flat
- a bungalow
- detached

- semi-detached
- terraced, or
- has any unusual features

> **TIP:** Ex-council houses and properties above premises can be tricky. Fewer lenders like them, so you'll limit the number of lenders who will consider your application. You'll remember at the beginning of the book, whenever something limits the number of lenders, it tends to increase the interest rate and your monthly cost.

Freehold/leasehold

If you're purchasing a leasehold property, it means that you don't own the building. This mostly applies to flats and apartments. A key consideration is how long the lease has to run at the time of purchase, and when the mortgage will end. Most lenders like you to have a minimum of thirty-five years remaining on the lease at the end of the mortgage term.

If you own the freehold then you own the building. Most houses are freehold.

Location

For some, location is more important than the property you're buying. You need to consider things like commuting time, how close your family are, and distance to other important amenities like shops, hospitals and public transport.

There are other little things to consider, too. What's the

traffic like? Google Maps has an excellent tool to tell you what the average traffic is like on roads at different times of the day. This is an invaluable tool when you're only free to view properties at lunchtime, for example. Are you on the right side of town? How much does this matter to you now? What about in the future, if you'll be changing jobs?

There are a few other things that you'll definitely want to know about before you move in. Depending on the location, you might discover that the village in question is full of holiday lets, so it will be empty most of the year – completely removing any sense of community in the area.

You might also want to look out for any major developments that could be crowding the horizon in the near future. New developments are popping up all over the place. Check with the council to see if there could be one in the area you like.

You might also want to think nationwide – would you consider moving a long way away? Property up in the north of the UK (not necessarily Scotland) tends to be cheaper than down south. What could get you a one-bedroom flat in London could get you a four-bedroom mansion if you look further north, for example. (Active Brokers has a handy blog post all about the difference in house prices up north and how to beat the high prices down south. You can read it at http:// activebrokers.co.uk/5-ways-to-beat-high-property-prices/)

Schools

This might not be relevant to you right now, or at all. But it's something you should consider. Do you want to live in a neighbourhood popular with young families? Does that sound perfect or nightmarish? Think about the future, check out the catchment areas, and take a look at things like the desirability of the schools in the area.

With this information, you might be able to predict where your future children will go to school if you decide to live in this location. Try to imagine growing up in this location: is there plenty to do for toddlers, school-age children, teenagers? All of these are important considerations if you're moving into a new home for the long term.

How to decide if it's 'the one'

Prioritise

You need to divide all the features you're looking for into two columns: essentials vs luxuries. For example, it's essential to be within commuting distance of your work, but being close to the local takeaways is a luxury. So, when you're looking for the right location for properties, you can instantly narrow it down to ones that meet your essential needs first, and then consider the luxuries after.

If you prioritise right from the beginning, then you'll end up with a property that meets all your needs perfectly, fits within your budget, and won't leave you in a nightmare position.

Once you've decided on these points and found a property, here are a few more tips to help you make up your mind.

Close scrutiny

Getting an appropriate survey doesn't come until later in the mortgage process, so looking out for potential problems could help you eliminate a few properties before you've even started the process. Don't forget to look out for damp in the property, any cracks (other than hairline ones), and any other obvious defects – try to find out how serious they are.

You'll also want to find out how old the roof is and what other parts of the house might need a lot of work in the years to come. Take plumbing, for example: it might be working fine now, but if it's already a decade old when you're buying the property, it might not be long until you need to fork out to redo it completely.

Don't forget to check on how much storage space there is, and don't underestimate how much you're likely to need, especially if you have a growing family.

Do your research

This might sound a bit odd, but it's often a good idea to drive around the property and the neighbourhood at different times of day, or year (if you've got ages to decide). Discovering that the pub a few doors down has loud live music late into the night could be a deal breaker. This is why it's important to get the feel of the neighbourhood before you move there permanently.

There are plenty of places online where you can find details like the crime rates in the area, reviews of the local restaurants, ratings for local schools etc. And you might be able to browse the local newspaper online, which is another way of getting the flavour of an area. It's also a good idea to do some research offline, too. Chat with the neighbours *before* you move in. The neighbours will know better than anyone the problems on that street, what the council is like, who makes the most noise in the morning, whose cat to avoid... Talk to them beforehand, get in their good books, and find out if you really want to buy this property. Furthermore, the neighbours are likely to be living in a property structurally very similar to yours. They might have some insights on any problems to prepare for when it gets cold, or where the damp is most likely to creep in.

If you can, find out why the property is up for sale. It might be something as innocent as the family outgrowing their home ... or it could be a serious problem with the layout of the house that won't be obvious until you move in.

Also check on what the Wi-Fi is like at the property, whether it's prone to power outages, or in a flood-prone area, or even if it could be at risk from coastal erosion. Other things you should check in advance include the bills you'd have to pay in the new home – will they represent a huge increase on what you're currently paying?

So – a lot to think about before you finally commit...

Summary

Consider the best type of property for you, both in terms of your needs, and what is likely to be acceptable to a lender: some will not lend on ex-council properties or flats above commercial premises. If you're considering a leasehold property, find out how many years remain on it.

Do your research on the location you have in mind: you'll want to know about schools, traffic, building plans, etc. Chat with your potential neighbours and get to know the area. (For me, having a shop within walking distance has been very important, especially with small children.)

Chapter 8
BUILDING YOUR DREAM HOME

Building your own property can seem very attractive, particularly if you're struggling to find a property that measures up to your expectations. Whether you buy, build or buy and rebuild, it's your decision and you need to have all the facts.

A self-build home is just that: a home that you build yourself – an opportunity to build the perfect property for your needs, based on your designs and ideas. Many self-builders will hire a project manager to oversee the on-site contractors, but make no mistake, you will have full control over the process.

Self-building involves finding land to develop, deciding on the home you want from either existing designs or having an architect design plans to your specification, arranging the right project management support to oversee the build, and actually building your new home (or more likely having it built).

Building from your own plans gives you total flexibility, but this carries a cost and sometimes too much choice can be a bad thing. Buying ready-made plans for a chosen property type can be an ideal option for some who want tighter guidelines to work to, but you may be restricted to a design that fits your plot. Whichever you choose, you'll have plenty of options, from the layout to the orientation of your home on its plot, to interior and exterior decor.

Mortgages for self-build properties work a bit differently from other residential mortgages. The principle is still the same: you approach a lender, the lender gives you a loan and then you pay back that loan over a stated term each month with interest added (if it's a repayment mortgage). However, to get that loan from the lender not only do you have to pass affordability tests and have a deposit, but you also need to show detailed plans for how you'll build the property and what the costs to maintain it will be. Once you get approval, the lender will release the funds to you in stages so you can pay for the various stages of your project.

Does this sound complex? Self-build mortgages do take some time to understand, but it could all be worth it if the pros outweigh the cons.

Pros of self-build

The biggest attraction to self-building is the prospect of having a property exactly how you want it. The prospect of being able to place every brick exactly where you want it, designing every room the perfect size for its purpose, and landscaping your fantasy garden is what pulls many people through the long (and often tricky) self-build journey. Furthermore, self-building means you should be able to build your home in the perfect location – assuming you can find the land. Read on to find out why finding the perfect spot can be difficult, though.

Many self-builders feel that their method can work out cheaper. The value of your finished property could be higher than the cost of building it, meaning you've made a saving. You can also make future savings by picking out specific materials and fittings for your home that reduce running costs, such as installing solar panels at the building stage along with other energy efficiency measures. You have the opportunity to build your home with the future in mind, so make sure that you build it efficiently to keep costs down.

Cons of self-build

Self-building can take a long time. Not only can living somewhere else while you build your new home drain your money, but over the months or years it takes to get your new home completed, so much could change. Another child? Financial crisis? Family issues? Anything could happen during the time it takes to build a home, potentially leading to delays, or, worse, abandoning the project.

Building your own home, of course, requires a huge amount of planning. You can hire a project manager to oversee all the building on the site and make sure everything runs on time, but that carries a cost. Many self-builders find the planning never stops. As each new stage of the build starts, it brings with it more decisions that need to be made. It can sometimes feel like one enormous juggling act to make all the ends meet – and still things could go wrong, especially if you don't have any professional input for your plans and ideas. Mortgage lenders will want to see that professional advice, planning and management are present throughout your project, so they know precisely how much money you'll need at each stage and why.

Is this a good place to build your home?

Finding the right place to build your home can sometimes be a nightmare. There's only so much land available to buy in the UK, and there's no guarantee that it will be suitable to build on. You'll need to consider the local amenities, whether the right schools are in travelling distance, what the Wi-Fi will be like, energy networks, clean and waste water, how close the shops are and, oh, don't forget the neighbours.

You could end up building a home in a neighbourhood of people you just don't get along with, but if a property does not exist on the land right now, no-one knows what the locals will be like! Furthermore, future changes to government rulings could mean that your idyllic rural retreat may one day have a large housing estate built right next door. Don't, forget that even if you can build your house exactly how you want it, it might not be in the place you imagined. For some people that might ruin the idea of a self-build property entirely.

There's a lot of red tape to navigate around when building your own home. Getting planning permission alone can take eight to twelve weeks, or perhaps even longer if your application is complex. Then there are building regulations and environmental surveys to consider. You'll need to address

- structural safety
- fire safety
- resistance to contaminants
- toxic substances
- ventilation
- sanitation
- hot water
- waste disposal
- heating and appliances
- conservation
- glazing
- electrical safety

… the list goes on.

It's not just a case of ticking those things off; you need to be seen to be complying with all the regulations: inspections take place throughout the build until the final sign off. If you skip any of this, you could be fined £5,000 or forced to re-do the entire build. As the owner of the property, it falls to you to make sure everything is compliant.

People may not want to buy your bespoke home when you come to move. The more unique your property is and the more it satisfies your specific needs, the more limited market you could have to sell it on to. Many buyers like putting their own touches onto properties (which makes perfect sense –

isn't that why you're looking into building your own?), so when they see your very unique, very personal property, it can be a bit off-putting. Of course, this all depends on how well you display and market your property when it comes to the sale – getting it in front of the right people is essential.

How do I decide if self-build is for me?

Would you consider a renovation instead of a home build? The important thing is to think realistically! Plan your dream home sensibly – you do need to live there once it's built, after all.

Consider each stage of the self-build project in detail, and imagine yourself going through the self-build process. Ask yourself: will the project be a success? Will it be stressful to manage alongside your work and family life? Building your own home has its foundations (see what I did there?) in your goals. Will this house give you the flexibility and freedom to grow and flow with the demands of the life you want to lead? Always keep in mind that this project must suit you for the long term; it doesn't just end when the build is complete. Maintaining the property and selling it in the future should be considered before you even start.

Consider all the options you have available to you. In some areas, self-building will mean moving miles away to find a plot of land. Instead, would you consider renovating or converting an existing property?

In any case, start by defining your goals. Decide what you ultimately need in a property and figure out what other things you desire but could sacrifice if necessary. From this point, you can start to make plans and research more in depth what is possible for your budget, needs, area and other circumstances.

It's a good idea to start drawing up the plans you would show a lender, as a test to see if you could really handle building a property.

(If you need any assistance with working out how much money you need, and if lenders will be willing to lend you this, give Active Brokers a call so one of our advisers can run through things with you.)

Summary

You need to consider the pros and cons of self-build carefully and ask yourself whether you are ready for a long wait before you can move into your dream home. Most lenders will release funds in stages, as the work is completed, and you need to bear in mind that you will have to cover your accommodation costs while the house is being built.

You also need to weigh up the total amount of funding required for the project against the end value of the property: a very individualistic building shaped entirely round your tastes and needs may not find many buyers when you come to sell it.

Finally, red tape is a massive consideration. There are numerous building and environmental regulations you have to comply with, or you are at risk of having to restart the build completely at your own expense.

PART 5
Victory

My Story
APPLYING FOR THE MORTGAGE

Now we had our offer on the property accepted it was down to my adviser to submit the application. As I can't provide myself with mortgage advice, I had been working with one of my adviser to get the job done.

The first step was to verify my identity and Ayesha's, which meant providing passports and driving licences. The lender also requested three months of business bank statements, as well as three months' personal bank statements, and my company accounts.

I knew from initial conversations right back at the beginning, when I was hunting for the right lender, that they would want to write to my accountant to get an accountant's reference. Having been through the process over 200 times with so many different self-employed scenarios, I now understand a great deal about lenders' expectations and the questions they may ask, hence the need for this book – although we still get faced with new ones every week. Adopting a logical approach is the best tactic.

On seeing my company accounts, the lender asked why there had been an increase in profits in the previous / latest year. I was able to answer that I had reduced our lead / marketing costs, and that as the business had been trading for a great deal longer we were getting more referrals and recommendations than ever. The accountant could see that in the accounts, and I was to answer some other questions with justifiable explanations. (I see on a lot of accounts that the turnover is the same but profits have increased in the most recent year. The usual explanations for this is that in the previous year the applicants bought premises or machinery, or invested in new systems or extra staff for the business. When these sort of expenses drop out of your accounts, it will increase the amount you make year on year, so it's usual for a mortgage lender to question it.)

The whole process, from application to providing all the documentation to having a survey on the property, took seventeen days. Our mortgage offer duly arrived, and at this stage the job was done, however, there is still a considerable amount of work to do. My administrator was constantly on the phone not only to my solicitor, but also to the estate agents to ensure that the other party's solicitors were doing everything they needed to do as quickly as they needed to do it.

It entailed a fair bit of legwork by my administrator as I had her contact them regular, but it meant I had complete clarity that everything was heading in the right direction. Having an administrator saved me a great deal of time because I only spoke to my solicitor once, and I let my administrator Lauren manage the whole process from application submission through to completion and just keep me updated.

As a business owner, and with other clients to help, I didn't have the time to be chasing my own mortgage application. In the end, the process I went through was relatively easy, but we have seen from over 200 client applications we have worked with that the process can be very slow, frustrating and time-consuming. There is a huge advantage to using an adviser who offers to be your one point of contact and chase your solicitor. It means they take care of any potential problems or delays when they arise. The amount of trouble-shooting and problem solving my team do at this stage is insane, but often our client doesn't even know about them because they are resolved immediately.

My exchange and completion would have taken a lot longer if my team hadn't taken care of it – and this is now part of the service we provide to my clients. The whole process was done and dusted within thirteen weeks – but it was thirteen weeks of pain, of stress, of worry.

On the flip side, this exercise completely transformed our business. It developed the knowledge I'm now able to pass on to you. Had I not been through this stressful time, you wouldn't be reading this guide today.

Chapter 9
THE APPLICATION PROCESS

Your adviser's goal is to simplify the application process for you. This can be a daunting and anxious time for you, particularly if you are a first-time buyer. An adviser's job is to provide reassurance, offer assistance, put your mind at ease, and hold your hand throughout the process.

The application is broken down into two key stages: pre-offer and post-offer.

Pre-offer

It's the sole responsibility of your adviser to get you from initial conversation to mortgage offer. Once the mortgage offer is produced, the baton is generally passed to your solicitor, who will take care of the rest of the process, right up until you move into your house. A good adviser will have a process in place for liaising with estate agents and solicitors to ensure the mortgage is completed in the shortest possible time.

> **TIP:** Typically, it takes fifteen to thirty working days from application to offer. It can take as little as ten days or as long as sixty days in the most extreme cases I have had. Ask your adviser to provide you with an estimate based on your circumstances and also lender timescales.

The period from application to offer is very labour-intensive. It involves up to ten hours of discussions with lenders. Ask your adviser if they will provide you with a dedicated mortgage administrator to handle processing your application. This speeds the process up.

The application process is very simple and generally comprise the following stages:

1. Your adviser submits your application submission.
2. Further client documents maybe required.
3. The lender to assess the documents you provided to your adviser and requests the relevant references, for example, from your employer or accountant.
4. The valuations/surveys take place.
5. Further checks take place. From time to time we have seen more documents requested at this stage in complex cases.
6. The lender produces a mortgage offer.

Documentation you will need to supply

Although your adviser will do most of the work for you, they still need you to give them the initial information to get things started. I feel it is better for your adviser to request as much as possible as early as possible in the process, to be more accurate with the advice provided and save hassle later on. Once the application is submitted, the underwriter may request more information, because a decision is dependent on an accurate picture of your circumstances.

Your adviser will hopefully anticipate what the underwriter may need. Having to go back and hunt through your files repeatedly, rather than just once thoroughly, is a frustration they would prefer to spare you.

Proof of identity and address

When people apply for mortgages, they need to prove their identity and address. This is a precaution to combat money laundering. Even though we live in an electronic world many mortgage lenders still require the adviser to certify that they have seen the original identification. If you receive your statements and bills electronically, you will need to contact your utility company or bank and ask them to post bill/statement.

Your adviser will tell you what they require, but bear in mind you may need to send your proof of identity and address using tracked delivery. Once your adviser receives your documents, they should copy, certify and return them immediately, again by recorded trackable post. Your ID must be in the name you have used to apply for the mortgage. We have seen instances where a passport has not been updated and is still in a maiden name; this can cause delay as it does not verify your identity.

Ask your adviser if they are able to certify your ID and address. This means they can send additional certified copies to your solicitor, which will make your life easier.

If you're completing a postal or email application and your adviser has not met you face to- face, you must provide two forms of identity and two proofs of address (usually utility bills or bank statements) to comply with anti-money laundering legislation.

> **TIP:** If you are living with parents or a partner and have no utility bills in your name, please see link below for additional proofs of address

To download a list of commonly acceptable ID and address visit: www.activebrokers.co.uk/book

Proof of income and profits

Usually you need to provide your last two years' accounts or Tax Calculations. Where applicable, some lenders may request a third year from you. Company accounts generally show the last two years company figures, so in essence the lender is able to see the last three years. Any significant increase in profits looks especially good in the eyes of your lender and, as mentioned previously, I really like to know as much as possible about the reason for any and all increases or significant changes.

But equally, business isn't always rosy. If there has been a decrease in your latest year, then it's likely that it's those figures that will be used for calculating your affordability (see Chapter 3).

Accountant's proof of income

Some lenders don't require accounts and instead rely on an accountant's reference letter. Your adviser should have a template for this. Some lenders will send this request directly to your adviser, who should also offer to work with your accountant on your behalf to complete this template.

I like to speak to accountants as much as possible, not only to save you time and stress but also because I believe that, where applicable, explanations from accountants about business scenarios are key to success.

Pay slips

If you are employed or employed by your partner you are going to need a minimum of three months' payslips and in some instances six. If you are paid weekly, then I am afraid you will need to dig out the last twelve weeks' payslips.

Case study: pay slip problems

One client of mine, Donna, had the wrong tax code on her pay slip.

We found this out when, after sending all her documents to the lender, they reduced the amount she could borrow by £30,000, which would have meant she and her partner would not have been able to buy their dream house. We spent approximately five hours on the phone to the lender, HM Revenue and Customs, the client and her payroll department to resolve the error.

A new payslip had to be produced, but we did get her that all-important offer for the required amount.

Online bank statements

Check with your adviser whether your lender will accept online bank statements. If you need to print out online bank statements, make sure they show your name, address, account number and sort code. The lender will want to see all your transactions within a specific time period. Don't provide summaries; they need the full details. If your bank statements do not show name, address, account number and sort code as well as the transactions, they will not be accepted

Three personal bank statements

In some instances, lenders may only require one month's bank statements. In others – in the case a newly self-employed person with a lower deposit, say – this could be six months' worth. Check with your adviser whether you lender will accept online statements. Be aware that if you request these directly from your bank, it can delay your mortgage offer.

Statements must always show full months. If you're printing out online statements covering three months, make sure you don't have any gaps in your transactions.

Three business bank statements

From time to time a lender may request a business bank statement, and they most certainly will if you are applying for a commercial mortgage. The requirements are very much the same as for personal bank statements. A request for business bank statements is much more common when you're relying on limited company profits to prove your income. The lenders want to see how well the company finances are run. Whether using paper or online statements, again, make sure there are no gaps. Be sure to include your

- company name
- business address
- account number
- sort code

> **TIP:** If you have requested bank statements from in branch and your branch have stamped them, this does not constitute verification. If your adviser has requested originals, that is what they will need to see.

The offer

Receiving your mortgage offer is the most important moment in the whole process; it's the point when you can relax and be happy that you have the mortgage in the bag.

You and your solicitor will receive a copy of the offer, and that means the mortgage adviser's job is complete. Everything is then in the hands of the solicitor, who will get you through to moving-in day.

> **TIP:** Exchange and completion can happen on the same day. This is more common with remortgages.

Summary

Your adviser will submit your mortgage application, and your documents will be assessed by the lender, who may ask for further documentation, and may write to your accountant. .

These are the essential pieces of documentation you will need to be able to supply:

- proof of identity (see www.activebrokers.co.uk/book)
- proof of address (see www.activebrokers.co.uk/book)
- sole trader: April tax calculations and tax year overviews or company accounts for the last two years
- Limited company director: last two years' April tax calculations and tax year overviews or company accounts for the last two years
- employed: three months' payslips
- credit report
- bank statements for the most recent three months, showing income credit, main personal spend, and mortgage/rent payments where applicable
- proof of deposit, usually in the form of a bank statement (lenders will sometimes want to see where funds are coming from, for example, if a deposit is coming from savings they will sometimes want to see a build-up of funds)
- all existing insurance schedules /and policy details,

including life insurance, critical illness cover, income protection, and home and health insurance.

If someone has been trading for less than a year or if the current tax year is coming to an end, I also like to see, for a sole trader, a projection of net profits, or for a limited company director, management accounts or their gross profit, net profit, salary and dividends.

The property will also receive a valuation. It takes on average seven to thirty days for a mortgage application to be accepted and an offer produced. During this time your mortgage adviser and/or their administrator should chase up the application and, keep you updated throughout the process.

Your mortgage offer is sent to you, your solicitor and your adviser.

Chapter 10
THE EXCHANGE

This is when you sign the contract for your new home. The exchange is your final hurdle – and it can be a little stressful waiting around for solicitors to complete the sale and / or purchase.

In most cases, it can take anywhere between seven and twenty-eight days for the exchange to be completed. In some cases, it is possible to complete the exchange on the same day, but this can be risky. You become vulnerable as not only can the seller make last-minute demands, but you're also relying on all the money being transferred on time.

This final stage is managed solely by solicitors acting on behalf of the buyer and seller.

Once a contract has been signed for exchange, it's very difficult for a buyer to back out. Exchanging contracts means you are legally bound to buy the property.

Selling a property in England and Wales

Agreement

Once the sale has been agreed, your solicitor will

- gather your title deeds
- prepare and send you a legal information package and a contract of sale
- request a settlement figure for your mortgage plus other secured loans
- converse with all relevant parties involved in the exchange
- negotiate a date for moving (set the 'completion' date)

Exchange

Once the contracts have been exchanged, your solicitor will

- receive the deposit as the down-payment on the property
- prepare the final settlement for your approval
- collect any funds required
- arrange for the deed transfer and for you to sign it

Completion

Once the exchange has been completed, your solicitor will pay off the mortgage, notify the Land Registry, and hand the deeds over to you, or more likely your mortgage lender.

Buying a property in England and Wales

Agreement

Once the sale has been agreed, your solicitor will organise searches of the local authority on your behalf, request your deposit; and deal with the formal mortgage offer.

Exchange

Once contracts have been exchanged, your solicitor will hand over the deposit to the seller's solicitor, prepare the final completion statement (which needs your approval), and collect any balance needed.

Completion

Upon completion, your solicitor will receive and arrange payment of any stamp duty; prepare and send off an application to the Land Registry; and send the deeds to the lender (if the property is mortgaged).

PART 6

Entrepreneurial

My Story
WHAT THE FUTURE HOLDS

Once you own a dream home your property journey doesn't have to stop there. If your business dream is to become a property investor then owning a residential property could make it a lot easier for you.

Investing in property is a passion of mine and involves buying and selling at the right times, reviewing your interest rates regularly, and looking at ways to increase the value or the number of properties you own to receive a passive income. This is all part of being entrepreneurial with property.

I review my mortgage regularly when my interest rate deal comes to an end by comparing my existing lender's interest rate with those of new lenders to make sure I have the most suitable and cost-effective mortgage at all times.

This could also be a good time to enhance the property's value, by perhaps raising/releasing some equity if the property value has already increased. We bought our home because of the potential to convert the garage into a utility room and the loft into a fifth bedroom with en-suite and walk-in wardrobe. The cost of making the change to our home will be far less than the value they add, which gives us an increased amount of equity which we can use to invest in a new, bigger property.

There are many different ways to invest in property, some of which I have personal experience of through my investment strategy, and other mechanisms that I have arranged for my clients.

I am really passionate about property, because I believe having assets that generate a passive income are the key to financial freedom and better choices in life. Having worked with and helped many property investors I know having the right strategy is important, and this is really where my skills lie.

As a property investor, I have a separate business with a business partner who is an expert in property, refurbishments and lettings. We have decided on the right strategies for us, which include:

- houses in multiple occupation
- commercial conversions
- land development
- using joint venture finance as well as mortgages

Our joint venture partners are clients, friends and family who we know and/or have worked with previously. In today's economy of low interest rates, any savings or large sums of money in the bank are earning our joint venture partners very little (whereas Alan Sugar in 2017 enjoyed a £181m dividend from his property portfolio).[1]

---

1. http://www.telegraph.co.uk/business/2017/01/08/lord-sugar-enjoys-181m-dividend-property-empire/

Property, I feel, is the ultimate compounding approach and has the potential to generate a guaranteed income right the way through retirement, leaving a legacy in the process. (This is just my opinion, not my advice – as ever, you should seek your own advice relevant to your circumstances.). To me it is simple: compare the value of a house fifty years ago with its value today.

Chapter 11
EXPLOIT THE VALUE IN YOUR PROPERTY

Why is this section entitled 'Entrepreneurial'? In simple terms, because it looks at how you can make money from your property and offers some useful lessons on property investing. There are many different avenues you could go down. In this section, I am going to show you how to make your property work as hard as you do.

Remortgaging

Hopefully you know by now that when you first take out a mortgage you're generally tied into a deal, that is, a fixed or variable interest rate, as described earlier in the book. That will be for a specific period of time, say, two, three, or five years.

When that deal comes to an end, the lender is going to usually put you on to their standard variable rate. This can be much higher than the original deal. Ideally, your existing lender will offer you a new interest rate to bring your payments back down, because the increase from a fixed rate to the standard variable rates usually sees your payment increasing. This is also an ideal time to check the market and speak to an adviser for comparisons.

Remortgaging is simply going to a new lender and comparing what they have to offer against what you're being offered by your current lender. It's a bit like doing a balance transfer on a credit card – you always want to maintain the lowest rate of interest on any form of debt.

Remortgaging is an opportunity for you to review your circumstances, and at this stage you have a few options. You could:

- reduce the mortgage term if you can afford to pay more
- pay off a lump sum, usually without penalty
- increase your mortgage to raise equity which could be used to add value to your home (of which more in the next section)
- increase your mortgage to borrow a deposit on your first investment property i.e. buy to let or increase your mortgage to buy a property abroad

Raising capital

When it comes to increasing your mortgage, you may think that you can afford it and that it will be a simple process.

However, you will usually have to apply and do everything I have already described. Some lenders will set a limit based on the value of your property and can query why you'd want to borrow more.

If you are looking to raise money for home improvements, lenders like to see estimates of the work to be carried out. Having these in advance will speed up the process and simplify your application.

It may be possible to raise up to 90% of your property value. If you're unable to do so with your current lender, you have the option to look at a second mortgage, that is, a secured loan, which I'll cover in the next chapter.

For self-employed people, a secured loan or second mortgage can be a significant opportunity. If your circumstances have changed drastically, getting a remortgage might not be possible. The alternative option that you could potentially consider if you want to increase the amount of your mortgage is a second mortgage, or a secured loan, as they're also known. It sits behind your main mortgage, so you apply for it in exactly the same way. The lender does all the same checks and have the same requirements when it comes to affordability.

Let me illustrate this with a client case study.

Case study: getting a better deal with a second mortgage

I had a client with substantial net assets. His residential mortgage was interest only and he wanted to loan for £200,000 which will allow him to carry out his renovations and gain the extra income every month as soon as the property is rented out.

Second mortgages also have some extra flexibility, in that you can borrow up to six times your income (as outlined in the 'income multiples' section in Chapter 3).

The reason it's called a second mortgage is because if your house were to be repossessed, mortgage lender A would be paid off first and the person who had the second mortgage or the secured loan would be paid off afterwards. Now, if the house were sold at a much more reduced priced, there might not be enough money to pay off all of the second mortgage or the secured loan. You will find, therefore, because there's extra risk for that type of provider and that type of lender, that the interest rate will be somewhat higher than for the first mortgage.

Second mortgages really are a great option if you want to increase your borrowing. You can often get quite high income multiples: getting six times your income is achievable, for any number of reasons on a secured loan. Lenders are a little bit more flexible in terms of what they will do to lend to you in this context.

Adding value to your property

Adding value to your home needs to be undertaken carefully, and ideally you will have chosen a property that you can ultimately develop over a period of time. One of the things to look for is somewhere that has the opportunity to build over the garage or extend at the back. Adding square footage to your home will definitely increase the value of your property.

There are also four key improvements you can make:

- upgrading your current windows
- upgrading the kitchen
- improving the bathrooms
- adding that important square footage – perhaps by converting your garage into another room

All these things will add value to your property itself – and to your home while you live in it, of course. The more money you can make from the property you're in, the more it will give you to invest in other properties or use as deposit on a much larger property.

For a very small investment, or for a large investment if you're doing a complete property development, you could almost double your return, providing you're happy to put up with the headache of doing it all.

The 'This Is Money' website pulled together some great figures on how much improvements can add to your property. Renovating it can be a good way to help make your current property better suit your needs, meaning there's no need to move house at all. Such renovations and home improvements also help to increase the value of your current property, meaning that your home could sell for much more, allowing you to find your dream home with a bigger deposit.

Home improvement	Average cost	Added value
Loft conversion	£15,000–£40,000	10%
Extra bathroom	£2,500–£6,000	6.1%
New kitchen	£8,000	5.8%
Central heating	£3,235	5.4%
Conservatory	£4,000–£10,000	5%

Chapter 12
INVESTMENT PROPERTIES

You don't have to be a full-time property developer to make owning property one of your income streams, and it can be an ideal source of extra revenue for the self-employed. Below are some ideas for how to make the most out of your current property, as well as invest in further property.

Let-to-buy

Let-to-buy is the situation that arises when you already own your own home and want to go and buy another property, perhaps because, although you like the property you're in at the moment, it's not quite big enough.

In my own case, the value of our property had increased quite considerably, so we had a fair bit of equity. What we'd actually like to have done is remortgage, and put our existing home on to a buy-to-let mortgage. By doing this, we could raise a little bit of extra money to put down as a deposit on a new property. That would mean we were going to let our existing property and buy a new one to live in ourselves.

In this situation, the existing mortgage that you are changing to a buy-to-let mortgage is determined by the amount of rent the property will fetch. Income is taken into account, which I cover below, but it doesn't impact the amount you can borrow for the new home you plan to move into. The mortgage on a buy-to- let is mostly based on the rental yield of the property. See below for buy-to-let information.

The new mortgage for the house you are moving into will be based on the factors we have been discussing throughout this book.

Becoming a landlord

Buy-to-let

If you want to stay in your home and buy an investment property as a buy-to-let, then that is completely different. You will be buying a property for investment, and everything will depend on the rental income that you're going to receive. The rent will determine how much you can borrow as a mortgage.

Deposits are a crucial factor when looking at either a buy-to-let or a let-to-buy. Most mortgage lenders like you to have at least a 25% deposit. With a 25% deposit the majority of mortgage lenders will be prepared to offer you a mortgage providing the rental income is adequate. There is a possibility, at the present time, of getting a mortgage with a 20% deposit, but the interest would be somewhat higher.

There is a very small number of lenders at the moment

who will offer a mortgage with a 15% deposit. What is annoying is that because there's a limited number of lenders who will take on that risk, their interest rates are significantly higher than for a 25% deposit. Providing you will still make money, it's certainly worth looking at these lenders if it suits your circumstances.

You should look at buy-to-let in two ways. If you're looking at it from the point of view of a short-term investment, you will want to make sure that you're receiving' say, £1,000 a month in rent, and that your mortgage payment is only going to be around £200 a month. You will actually be making a profit of £800 on a monthly basis. You want the money in the short-term and you're looking to include it in your income.

The other perspective is to view the buy-to-let as an investment property, or for your retirement income, providing you an income later on in life. The difference is with a short-term investment property on a buy-to-let, you would want the mortgage on an interest-only basis, to keep the payments as low as possible so you can keep the profit.

If you're looking to buy-to-let to provide you with an income in retirement, then it's best to have a mortgage that is going to paid off in twenty-five years, or by the time you reach retirement, so that you've got a pure asset and can actually start receiving income from the property.

If you have a number of properties, you could receive a significant income from them later on in life. Equally, if you come to sell those properties, there will to be no mortgages to repay, so you'll actually make more money out of them at that point in time as well. The real money is from the lump sum that you will get from the equity in the property.

Buy-to-let vs pension

This is a hot topic, so I am providing some basic FCA-compliant information. This information has been provided by pension expert Chris Clark, owner and managing director of www.advancewealth.co.uk.

Buy-to-let pros and cons:

On the upside:

- Your assets are diversified into property
- Your capital is retained (unlike with an annuity)
- There's good income opportunity as well as potential for growth

On the downside:

- The property can come at a high price
- Rental income isn't guaranteed – there may be periods without tenants
- You are liable for tax on the income
- You will have to pay for maintenance, and you have legal responsibility for the condition of the property
- Managing the property effectively can take up a lot of time
- Selling the property will incur a cost, and will take up time

Pensions pros and cons:

On the upside:

- There are excellent tax incentives with pensions
- You can choose a portfolio to suit your appetite for investment risk
- Pensions have good potential for growth over the long term
- You are in a favourable position when it comes to inheritance tax
- Pensions offer wide-ranging retirement options and liquidity

On the downside:

- The growth of a pension fund is not guaranteed
- The legislation on tax incentives could change
- You can't access a pension until you're fifty-five
- There is no guarantee of good annuity rates for the risk-averse

You should always speak to an independent financial adviser to ensure you're investing in line with your circumstances, objectives and your appetite for risk.

The standard warnings for both mortgages and pensions apply:

- Please note that, as a mortgage is secured against property, your home may be repossessed if you don't keep up repayments.
- Pensions are a long term investment and the capital

invested can go down as well as up. You may not get back the original amount invested.

Light refurb

Purchasing a property below market value, or something very run down, and improving it can be a great way to make money from property. This for some is known as 'flipping' a property.

Lenders tend to frown on the short-term use of mortgages, and if you are constantly taking out a normal mortgage and sell the property within a short period, it could impact on your ability to borrow.

Some lenders have a specific product to enable you to carry out light refurb work on a property; it is generally some form of bridging finance.

Houses in multiple occupation

With the return on investments they provide, it's easily to see why houses in multiple occupation (HMOs) are becoming increasingly popular as buy-to-let options.

The demand for affordable housing is increasing at an alarming rate in most large towns and cities. If you decide to rent by the room, it relieves the pressure the UK's housing stock is currently experiencing – and it could certainly bring you a handsome return on your investment.

So, HMOs provide affordable accommodation for tenants and increase the capacity of single dwellings to provide accommodation. In many cases, owners can expect double the yield from an HMO than they would get from a standard buy-to-let.

It's a fantastic business model where both sides of the equation are catered for. There's a rising demand as well as a rising supply – a perfect match!

There are two possibilities for a mortgage on an HMO:

1. The standard buy-to-let route, which considers the property value and the rent the property will achieve.
2. A commercial valuation, which is based on the income the property could generate. Generally speaking a commercial valuation, and therefore a commercial mortgage, allows you to increase the amount you can borrow.

Speak to an adviser about the two options and find out which suits your strategy best.

Serviced accommodation

Serviced accommodation is fully furnished accommodation available for both short- and long-term stays. It provides additional amenities not available in traditional rental accommodation.

I have found mortgages for serviced accommodation very hard to place with a lender, unless you have twelve months' experience of letting property or owning HMOs.

A serviced apartment will include:

• Wi-Fi
• dishwasher and washer/dryer
• fully-fitted kitchen
• linen and towels
• HDTV (or similar)

- Freeview TV Package
- housekeeping service

Some prospective tenants may also expect gym facilities and onsite parking.

Bear in mind that the longer someone is booking for, the more likely they are to expect to negotiate a lower nightly rate. You will also want to ensure that you have a cancellation policy that does not leave you out of pocket. Check the cancellation policy – they can vary a lot.

Commercial to residential conversion

This is the process of buying a commercial property and converting it into a home. One of the biggest benefits to this approach is that it's possible to secure a bargain. Prices for commercial properties can be significantly lower than those of residential new-build homes.

But before you rush out and begin bidding on a nearby warehouse, be aware of the particular considerations that arise with this type of property:

- The cost of labour – conversion of such properties often entails employing skilled workers
- The property could be subject to additional building requirements relating to fuel and power
- The access points to the original building could mean complications with parking

One major advantage we are seeing in 2017 is commercial property has no stamp duty payable.

Land development

Much of the information I supplied about self-build in Chapter 8 applies to buying land for building a single dwelling or multiple dwellings.

In order to undertake such a development, you need to purchase the land preferably with planning permission; not having it limits the number of lenders available and carries a huge amount of risk.

Once you have purchased the land, it may be possible to raise development finance to complete the build. What is important for the mortgage lender is the exit strategy after the property is built: how will these loans, which are often short term, be repaid? Will it be through

1. refinancing, or
2. sale of assets?

The key information you need when considering a development includes:

Address of the development –

- land title number (If you have it)
- copy of planning permission
- current value/purchase price
- build costs
- timescale for the project /end value/gross development value
- total amount of funding required
- amount required on Day One
- proposed exit route for borrowing
- details of any credit issues, if relevant –

I have seen the raising of deposits or the development being handled with a joint venture partner. It is key for a mortgage lender to understand you or your partner's experience of similar projects, so they may even request a CV outlining that experience.

Joint venture finance

This is a way of investing in property without using all of your own money.

When I join forces with a client or a joint venture (JV) partner the key thing I want them to understand is what makes me investable. The relationship is built on trust and honesty from the beginning. I have a property-focused business partner in my business because I am a finance expert rather than a property expert, so our values and skills complement each other perfectly and help our JV partners to make more money.

Why would a JV partner work with you?

If you had (lots of) money and you were busy and successful, would you get on the ground, learn everything about property or finance yourself, would you want to deal with solicitors, builders, estate and letting agents, doing it all yourself – or would you want someone else to take care of it all for you?

I find that the majority of the self-employed, and especially business owners, want to invest in property but are too busy or have no idea how, so if you have a great deal of knowledge in property it can be a great way to build your own portfolio as well as help your JV partners.

The key elements of helping a JV partner are:

- sourcing the property
- managing the build or refurb
- providing a share of the equity on sale or remortgage

The key elements your JV partner is looking for are:

- return on investment (ROI)
- an exit strategy – how they can get out if they want to
- security for their money
- most importantly, trust

The investors we generally work with put in the cash and we do the rest as we have the time, the team, the knowledge, and the experience.

We have many options available to suit our investors, and all the terms are agreed upfront, by which I mean that their share of the equity or the interest on the money borrowed from them represents a fixed rate of return. If you would like to learn more about JV finance or discuss being a JV partner then please get in touch.

Summary

Always remortgage when your deal ends to maintain the lowest interest rate. You can also use a remortgage or second mortgage – in effect, a secured loan – to raising capital. It can be used for various reasons, including to add value to your home: improved kitchens or bathrooms, new windows, or loft conversions, for example.

Property investment has many options, and owning a

property already can give you more access to lenders. Examples of property development include

- let-to-buy is the process of letting out the home you live in to buy and move into another house
- buy-to-let describes a property bought for the specific purpose of letting it out
- buy-to-lets vs. a pension: consider advice from a financial (pensions) adviser
- light refurb often entails getting short-term finance for the purpose of 'flipping' a property
- houses of multiple occupancy (HMO) are great for increased cash flow on properties
- serviced accommodation: lenders usually require you to have experience of buy-to- lets or HMOS
- commercial conversion is the process of buying an office or shop, or other business premises and converting them into residential properties. Finance can be arranged in on a short-term basis
- land development is buying land to build either single or multiple units on it. Finance can be arranged on a short-term basis
- JV finance entails using others' money for property investment

That brings us to the end of the entrepreneurial section of the book. I hope you have enough information now to feel confident on your options with property and more confident about going for a mortgage when the time comes.

Chapter 13
THE MORTGAGE JOURNEY

Thinking 12 to 24 months ahead of when you want to buy a property could really spare a lot of anxiety when you come to take the plunge.

The ACTIVE methodology really is your key to mortgage success.

This is the sequence of events that you, should expect, starting from when you speak to your adviser and this is the process my team follow.

STEP 1
Initial call to broker for a twenty to thirty minutes conversation

- where you are now: that is, value of any current property value, mortgage amount, deposits, fees
- where you want to be

- if now isn't the right time for you, we will inform you when will be
- you will get confidence, reassurance and hand holding
- confirmation of the process and our confirmed fees
- solicitor quotation provided along with summary email

STEP 2

The best documentation to have ready for you adviser is:

- in the case of a sole trader, the two years' April tax calculations and tax year overviews
- in the case of a director of a limited company, the last two years' April tax calculations and two years' company accounts
- accountant's name, address, email and phone number
- if employed, three months' payslips
- credit report (for a free one we recommend www .noddle.co.uk)
- the most recent three months' bank statements
- proof of deposit saved

Additionally, if you have been trading for less than one year, or if your current year is coming to an end, it is beneficial to get a projection of net profit if you are a sole trader, or a statement of gross profit, net profit, salary and dividends if you are the director of a limited company.

This is to make sure the advice and due diligence are completely accurate. The lender has a responsibility to assess your income and expenditure to make sure the mortgage is affordable.

STEP 3

Fact-finding requires a further thirty to sixty minute' conversation to complete fully, to establish

- personal details
- business, family and future aspirations and intentions
- appropriate insurance for your mortgage, family, health and home

STEP 4

Your adviser will usually research the market and complete all due diligence, and will also consider the most suitable interest rate and the most cost-effective mortgage.

Your adviser will provide full advice and recommendations for the lender, and the interest rates, and provide quotations.

My team email the confirmed lender to you and require an email back for acceptance to proceed to the next step.

If you are using the Active Brokers solicitor service, your dedicated administrator will complete all your chasing and be your one point of contact for both mortgage and solicitor.

This speeds up the completion (i.e. being able to move in), removes a great deal of stress for you, and simplifies the process for you.

STEP 5

Agreement in principle, that is, the credit check, is the first major step of the mortgage application, where your adviser will supply your information to the lender for initial assessment and acceptance.

STEP 6

Once you will have an agreement in principle certificate as confirmation of initial acceptance, you can proceed with finding your dream home and making a formal offer through an estate agent. Once your property offer is accepted we move on to the next step

To submit the application you will have to supply:

- property address
- estate agent's details
- If not using our solicitors the name, address and telephone number of your solicitor
- property details:
  - property type, including any unusual features
  - if it's flat, the number of floors in the building, the floor the flat is on and whether there is a lift
  - year of build
  - if leasehold, number of years remaining on the lease
  - any ground rent, service charges and insurance costs
  - number of bedrooms
  - number of living rooms
  - garage (single or double) or drive

As lenders require your most recent bank statement and payslips, you may need to provide additional ones if the previous five steps have taken a long time.

STEP 7

This stage is the full mortgage application, that is, the submission to the mortgage lender. When we submit the application, we will send you copies of the following:

- fact-find summary
- mortgage application
- the final quotation from the lender

We will also email declarations to be signed in relation to your application.

STEP 8

The lender assesses your income, affordability and the documentation we have provided them with. Once they have accepted this, the property valuation is done. During this time, we chase the lender continually and update you.

It takes on average 17 days to move to the next step.

STEP 9

Finally, you will receive the mortgage offer, that is, your offer of a loan from the lender; we will also check that your solicitor has also received a copy.

STEP 10

Your solicitor will arrange for exchange, which is taking legal ownership of the property, and completion, which means that you can move in.

How to achieve success

My team and I have helped everyone from property investors, to sole trader first-time buyers, to a multi-million pound business owner buying his third home for £5m, and plenty of clients with previous bad credit.

In my business, Active Brokers, we have had the best results for the following types of clients:

- those with two or more years' trading (and no previous year losses)
- those whose assets outweigh their liabilities on the balance sheet
- those with a 10% or more deposit
- people who have savings to cover the costs of buying/ moving
- those with a clear credit history for at least the last twenty-four months, i.e. no missed payments, defaults, CCJs etc.
- those with poor credit, but with 15% or more deposit
- People who have all their documentation ready at the beginning of the process (step 2 above).

To download the ACTIVE quick reference guide visit: www .activebrokers.co.uk/book

Acknowledgements

Ayesha, I am eternally grateful for your love and support – on a daily basis. Without you I wouldn't be the man I am and I thank you for always saying yes to my never-ending business ideas. You're an amazing wife and an even better mum. Thanks to my girls and our bump for always making me smile and being a constant reminder to be grateful for the life we share.

To my parents, Neil and Jo: no amount of thanks could ever be enough for always believing in me and showing me how to be a great man, parent and businessman. I realise now, as a father, how many of your lessons I took on and how they shaped me into who I am, not least the indirect business mentorship as I was getting as I grew up.

Thanks to the oldest members of the Active Brokers elite team: Jake Rogoff (mortgage adviser) for your trust, loyalty, support and advice over the years, as well as for the extra insights for the 'ACT' sections of the book; Lauren Tilly for providing exceptional customer support, exceeding expectations and assisting me with day-to-day operations, not to mention with the 'Victory' section; and Georgia Budd, for the insights in the insurance section – going from apprentice to insurance adviser in such a short space of time was exceptional and I have complete faith in your ongoing progress.

To the KPI legends Joy Zarine and Emma Mills, for the advice through the programme and for their ongoing friendship. I love seeing your journeys take shape.

A huge thank you to my clients, to everyone on social media who likes, comments and shares our posts, to those I've met at networking events and anyone who recommends the team and me to friends, family and colleagues. I am so grateful for the ongoing support, it all helps towards achieving our vision!

Thank you to Daniel Priestley for the KPI programme, and to the Dent community – without it I wouldn't have had the platform to share my message.

Finally, thanks to Lucy McCarraher and Joe Gregory for all your assistance with the book, the feedback, and getting it to publication.

Disclaimer

Please note the text contained within the book is for information purposes only and does not constitute advice. If you wish to discuss your mortgage or insurance policies or require advice in these areas you should contact a mortgage adviser who is authorised to give advice. You should contact a mortgage adviser for personalised advice for your specific circumstances. Please also ask us for a personalised illustration.

The Author

Gary Das is an entrepreneur and expert mortgage adviser with over fifteen years' industry experience. His speciality is helping sole traders, business owners, contractors, investors and entrepreneurs to navigate the mortgage minefield. Using the process laid out in this book helped  him to purchase his dream home and continue on his property investment journey to financial freedom.

Gary started out as a mortgage adviser at the Woolwich and worked for several large companies before becoming a self-employed mortgage adviser in 2006. When he and his wife decided it was time to move home in 2015, he was faced with regulation changes and post-credit crunch restrictions. He took on the challenge of sourcing the best mortgage available for them as a company director and his sole trader wife. His hours of research uncovered more flexible lenders and new knowledge that allowed him to increase his borrowing and move his family into their dream home.

Gary now works with sole traders, business owners, contractors, investors and entrepreneurs for 12 to 24 months before they want to buy, because the key really does lie in the preparation.

Gary's purpose is to safeguard the future of families for generations to come.

Active Brokers vision is for 4.6m self-employed people in the UK to have sanctuary and freedom in a home of their own and a mission to get property finance for you without being distracted from your business.

He believes that with the right planning and preparation you can have a dream life, including financial independence through becoming entrepreneurial with property, giving you the time and freedom to help others.

Connect with Gary Das

Facebook: Gary Das
LinkedIn: Gary Das
www.garydas.com

Connect with Active Brokers

Facebook: Active Brokers
YouTube: Active Brokers
www.activebrokers.co.uk